"A cutting-edge, comprehensive, and interactive approach to the science of addiction recovery, written with great respect and compassion for the reader. Anyone struggling with the demons of addiction will find real help here, and hope."

—**Terri Cheney**, author of the *New York Times* bestseller *M*

"*The Addiction Recovery Skills Workbook* is an excellent translation of modern science into practical skills development. From explaining the basic brain changes associated with the development of addiction to laying out a systematic path to behavioral change and recovery, Glasner-Edwards has taken the very best of addiction science and turned it into common sense and step-by-step instructions. I think this workbook will be as important for families and friends of addicted individuals as for those affected directly. Either way, this is a powerful and practical tool to aid recovery."

— **A. Thomas McLellan**, founder and chairman of the board of the Treatment Research Institute, and former deputy director of the White House Office of National Drug Control Policy

"In creating *The Addiction Recovery Skills Workbook*, Glasner-Edwards has developed a resource that is at the cutting edge of recovery from addiction. In a respectful, direct, and clear way, she provides readers with key tools necessary to build the motivation to change, learn the skills needed to change, and apply those skills to achieving and maintaining change. Glasner-Edwards does a wonderful job of integrating the three most critical innovations in evidence-based approaches to treatment in the last fifty years: cognitive behavioral therapy (CBT), motivational enhancement, and mindful observation. There has been excellent research in all three areas demonstrating their value in aiding individuals in achieving their goals to be clean and sober, and Glasner-Edwards has created a resource that will be a wonderful tool for anyone addressing substance use problems. I anticipate this workbook will become a standard in the field."

— **John R. McQuaid, PhD**, professor of clinical psychology at the University of California, San Francisco; associate chief of mental health for clinical administration at the San Francisco VA Medical Center; and coauthor of *Peaceful Mind*

"As one of America's most knowledgeable addiction scientists, Suzette Glasner-Edwards writes with clarity and authority about the state of the art of treatment for addiction, a devastating disease that affects millions of people and families. Glasner-Edwards explains the complex science of addiction in terms that everyone can understand. Most important, she provides guidance to help the afflicted overcome this illness. This book will help end the stigma of addiction and it will save lives."

— **David Sheff**, journalist and *New York Times* best-selling author of *Clean* and the memoir *Beautiful Boy*

"In this self-care book, Glasner-Edwards provides a much-needed addition to the substance abuse treatment field by providing a hopeful and highly accessible workbook for people struggling with substance abuse and addiction. This book explains the mystery of addiction and how to communicate with addiction treatment providers. It offers a range of interactive evidence-based therapy tools and techniques to achieve self-directed behavioral change. It integrates several important approaches, including cognitive behavioral therapy (CBT), mindfulness, and motivational interviewing, giving individuals powerful tools to tackle this devastating illness."

> —**Karen Miotto, MD**, clinical professor in the department of psychiatry and biobehavioral sciences at the University of California, Los Angeles (UCLA), and director of the UCLA Addiction Medicine Clinic

"I have worked in clinical addictions research for over fifteen years, and I can honestly say that this is no ordinary self-help workbook. Glasner-Edwards has expertly integrated the powerful combination of cognitive behavioral therapy (CBT), motivational enhancement, and mindfulness into an easily digestible treatment package that speaks directly to the person with an addictive disorder. It does more than just present a how-to guide to the implementation of these key, cutting-edge treatment strategies, however. This workbook also contains clear advice as to how, when, and where to ask for help; provides a framework for what is to be expected in the recovery process; and contextualizes the treatment strategies with other traditional addictions programs (12-step, medication, etc.). These particular inclusions mean that the workbook cuts across traditional, well-known barriers people report when considering addictions treatment, such as the stigma and mystery about what might happen, and problems with inconsistent, incoherent care. By integrating solutions that run across a range of lifestyle factors (e.g., exercise, social network enhancement, communication) and common comorbidities (e.g., depression, anxiety), this workbook also stands to be personally relevant to anybody concerned about their substance use, at any stage of severity. By hitting all of these targets sensitively, respectfully, and comprehensively in this workbook, Glasner-Edwards has provided a real service to the addictions community. I am going to recommend this to all of my clinical colleagues!"

> —**Frances Kay-Lambkin**, associate professor at the National Drug and Alcohol Research Centre at the University of New South Wales, Australia

THE
Addiction Recovery Skills Workbook

Changing Addictive Behaviors
Using CBT, Mindfulness, *and*
Motivational Interviewing Techniques

SUZETTE GLASNER-EDWARDS, PhD

NEW HARBINGER PUBLICATIONS, INC.

Publisher's Note

This publication is designed to provide accurate and authoritative information in regard to the subject matter covered. It is sold with the understanding that the publisher is not engaged in rendering psychological, financial, legal, or other professional services. If expert assistance or counseling is needed, the services of a competent professional should be sought.

Distributed in Canada by Raincoast Books

Copyright © 2015 by Suzette Glasner-Edwards
New Harbinger Publications, Inc.
5674 Shattuck Avenue
Oakland, CA 94609
www.newharbinger.com

Exercise 7.4, "SOBER Breathing," reprinted from MINDFULNESS-BASED RELAPSE PREVENTION FOR ADDICTIVE BEHAVIORS by Sarah Bowen, Neha Chawla, and G. Alan Marlatt, copyright © 2010 by The Guilford Press. Reprinted with permission of The Guilford Press.

Cover design by Sara Christian
Acquired by Tesilya Hanauer
Edited by Susan LaCroix

Library of Congress Cataloging-in-Publication Data

Glasner-Edwards, Suzette, author.
  The addiction recovery skills workbook : changing addictive behaviors using CBT, mindfulness, and motivational interviewing techniques / Suzette Glasner-Edwards ; foreword by Richard A Rawson.
     pages cm
  Includes bibliographical references.
  ISBN 978-1-62625-278-3 (paperback) -- ISBN 978-1-62625-279-0 (pdf e-book) -- ISBN 978-1-62625-280-6 (epub) 1. Substance abuse--Treatment. 2. Addicts--Rehabilitation. 3. Psychotherapy. 4. Meditation--Therapeutic use. I. Title.
  RC564.G45 2015
  362.29--dc23
                          2015030657

Printed in the United States of America

17   16   15

10   9   8   7   6   5   4   3   2   1   First printing

This book is dedicated to Lilly and Lila Edwards, for inspiring me to do all that I can to help people change; when we help one person heal, we slowly heal the world.

Contents

Foreword

I remember in the 1980s being told by a seasoned counselor that "clients" should not be educated about addiction, because it would allow them to feel like they could understand and "control" their drug use and this would interfere with their surrendering to their disease. For many years, addicted individuals in treatment programs were repeatedly told that they should shut up and just do what they were told. More recently, we hear celebrity endorsements for luxury treatment programs and quasi-religions which suggest that if you simply pay lots of money to these organizations and follow their science fiction or their narcissistically-inspired formulas, it is very possible to become "cured" and avoid the hard work of recovery. This is an attractive and seductive message, but an inaccurate one—it creates false hopes, but great profit margins. Both of these messages have been detrimental to the recovery efforts of many people.

In the development of effective, evidence-based treatments for people with health problems, including substance use disorders, a few fundamental principles have emerged. First, it is important to educate individuals with scientifically accurate information about their illnesses and about the steps they can take to improve their health. Second, it is important to empower these individuals to take action and become active participants in improving and maintaining their own health. Third, it is critical that information is conveyed to these individuals in a respectful way, not by talking down to them or being preachy or judgmental. Finally, to get people to use treatment materials, those materials need to be relatable, interesting, and realistic. All of these principles are important in giving people the tools they need to improve their health and make positive changes in their lives.

The Addiction Recovery Workbook reflects a sophisticated knowledge of how to effectively communicate to people struggling with substance use disorders. The workbook has been developed with a keen awareness of the scientific literature on the nature of addiction and the information and skills that are useful in helping people to stop using alcohol or drugs and develop a positive and sustainable recovery. The material in the workbook is presented in a way that shows a true understanding of how confusing, frightening, and discouraging addiction can be to individuals struggling with excessive alcohol or drug use. The book communicates its message in a respectful way, giving the readers credit for investing time and effort, for taking responsibility for their own lives, and for seriously wanting to make changes, while at the same time avoiding a condescending or paternalistic tone. In short, this book approaches readers as adults who are responsible for their own lives—who recognize they want to improve their lives, but are not sure exactly what to do or how to do it.

The reader is invited to join in the process of recovery, but, at the same time, it is clearly acknowledged that there may be ambivalence about taking on this job of recovery. *Is this whole recovery thing really necessary? Do I really have a problem with drugs or alcohol? Why does my intention to occasionally use slide into compulsive, sometimes catastrophic, out-of-control, excessive use? Am I crazy? Do I have self-destructive tendencies? Am I a bad person? I just want to be able to drink alcohol or use like a normal person—why does this go "sideways" when I try? How can I tell if I am addicted? What does it mean to be addicted?*

The first section of the workbook addresses many of the confusing and apparently paradoxical elements of addiction and how good, intelligent people can be drawn into a pattern of alcohol and drug use that can wreak havoc with their lives, resulting in damage to themselves and the people they love. This section contains current, accurate information about what addiction is, why some people get addicted and others don't, how to know if you do have a serious alcohol or drug problem, and what steps can be taken to begin to address this problem. The clear message is that there are many pathways and approaches to addressing problem alcohol and drug use. The workbook helps the reader understand that many people may need treatment with professional therapy, addiction medications, and 12-step support, and that the book can be used together with these other recovery tools and approaches.

All of this information is given with a recognition that the reader is in a state of ambivalence, which is natural and normal. Rarely do people dive into a program of recovery with a burning desire and deep commitment to changing their lives and giving up a set of behaviors that, at one point in their lives, was a great source of pleasure (and, at times, still is). As addiction is explained, many case examples and conversations are used to illustrate the salient points and to show readers that the workbook was written for people like themselves.

The heart of the workbook is a set of chapters that address the major aspects of the recovery process. Each chapter gives an overview of its main theme, using clear explanations of the scientific principles and processes involved, as well as lots of examples of how the issues it presents may relate to the reader's current situation. And each chapter has a wonderful collection of worksheets and written exercises to give readers a vehicle for expressing their own version of these issues and helping to personalize the concepts. These chapters cover an amazing array of the most current set of knowledge, principles, and skills that are considered either evidence based or extremely promising and under active study.

Included in these chapters are concepts of self-directed behavior change; all kinds of tools to help people modify thoughts and beliefs; ways to build rewards and positive new behaviors into a life in recovery; strategies for managing negative mood states and coping with cravings for alcohol or drugs; relapse prevention approaches and skills; and a format for creating a clear, simple, and practical recovery plan. The approaches and strategies in these chapters come from well-established clinical research literature. Included are concepts and skills from motivational interviewing, cognitive behavioral therapy, community reinforcement therapy, relapse prevention, contingency management, and the matrix model. In addition, other approaches are included that are currently considered to hold great promise in the addiction field but with more limited evidence. These include behavioral activation therapy, mindfulness meditation, dialectic behavioral therapy, and physical exercise.

Throughout the workbook, the principles and skills are illustrated with excellent case examples and scripts of conversations that help bring the information to life and make it useful. It is a very challenging task to communicate about the scientific literature on addiction and addiction treatment in a way that is accurate, understandable, and engaging. These case examples are written in such a way that they illustrate challenges, concepts, and solutions in a very readable style. What could otherwise be a litany of dry, clinical research is transformed into a collection of very relevant and applicable skills that readers can use and apply to their own situations. The sample conversation scripts help pull the readers into situations and allow them to vicariously get a sense of how it feels to manage these commonly experienced recovery scenarios.

The Addiction Recovery Workbook is an important new resource for individuals struggling with alcohol and drug use problems. It is an active document, not a textbook to be put on a shelf. The book has been written to enrich and empower the reader. For people who struggle with repeated failures to self-manage their alcohol and drug use, it is a refreshingly positive and hope-inducing resource. The overarching message is that there has been a great deal of knowledge amassed about the problem of addiction and there are many ways to make progress in achieving recovery. There is no one school of thought that has all the answers, and there is no "right way" to recovery.

The author clearly has great affection for the individuals she has worked with in her clinical practice and her research, who struggle with addiction. Her commitment to, and personal interest in, their well-being is conveyed on every page. *The Addiction Recovery Workbook* is her way of giving a gift of hope and assistance to others who struggle with alcohol and drug problems.

—Richard A. Rawson, Ph.D.
Professor and Co-Director
UCLA Integrated Substance Abuse Programs
Semel Institute of Neuroscience and Behavior
David Geffen School of Medicine
University of California, Los Angeles

Introduction

Imagine that you are driving a car. Normally, your brain tells you when to go and when to stop. If you see a green light quickly change to yellow as you approach an intersection, your brain tells you, *Hurry up, hit the brakes! There's danger here!* and almost instantly, without thinking, your foot is thrusting downward. The light turns red. You wait. The light turns green again. Your brain says, *Okay, go! It's safe now.*

There's a reason that your addiction is controlling you and your life, and not vice versa. You may know when to go and when to stop when you're driving a car, but research has shown very clearly that when you become addicted to alcohol or drugs, the part of the brain that tells you when to stop drinking or using drugs becomes impaired. It malfunctions—chronically. Terrible things can happen in your life as the result of your alcohol or drug use, but your brain becomes stuck in *go* mode. The brakes just stop working.

There are a range of circumstances that bring people into treatment for their addictions or to seek out a source of self-help, like this book. Maybe you've gotten into legal trouble; perhaps you've been arrested for driving under the influence. Yet even in the face of these hardships, your addicted brain says, *Go. Drinking will make you feel better.* Perhaps your alcohol or drug use has created conflict in one or more of your important relationships, whether with parents, a partner, your children, or others with whom you are close. Despite the hurt that your addiction has caused you and your family, your addicted brain says, *Go. Take a few pills; it will take the edge off. They just don't get it. You can control it if you really want to.*

Maybe your school or work performance has suffered, or you've even lost your job or dropped out of school or classes because of your alcohol or drug use. Your addicted brain says, *Go. You need to use to cope. If you don't use, you'll fall apart.* Another trigger point for seeking help is when your use of alcohol or drugs creates or worsens another condition. Maybe it used to make you feel better when you were depressed. But now drinking or using takes you to darker places than you ever could have imagined before this whole vicious cycle started. Your addicted brain says, *Go. Have a drink. You need it.*

There is a lot to learn about the addicted brain, and you will be an expert on your own addiction once you've read this book. But first, take a moment to congratulate yourself for overpowering the *go* response. If you're reading this book, that means that something inside of you is telling you to fight your addicted neurobiology. You had the intention to put on the brakes and find a way to reengage your brain's ability to say *stop*, and you acted on it. That intention usually comes from the recognition that the pain and suffering that your addiction has caused you and your loved ones now outweighs the good things that drinking or using once did for you.

As strong as that intention and recognition might be at this moment, the urge to return to drinking or using can be equally, if not more, powerful. You already know this, because you have tried to control your use before, but failed. Perhaps you have even quit before, but somewhere along the way, the urge to drink or use took you over and flipped the *go* switch back into place. It's that constant battle between the addicted part of the brain and the rational part of the brain that leaves those who suffer from addiction vulnerable to repeated episodes of destructive alcohol and drug use. These relapse episodes, while well understood as part of the illness, are often interpreted as a sign that recovery is not really possible to achieve. Some addicts reject the experience of an urge itself, feeling that urges are a sign that something is wrong or that they are not recovering.

Contrary to these ideas, scientific studies on the psychology of addiction have established that urges to drink or use drugs can persist well into recovery, and are not a sign of failure. As you learn more about the science behind addiction in this book, and as you practice three of the most effective therapeutic techniques for promoting recovery, you will develop an understanding of what an urge is and why it's happening to you, and you will be better equipped to cope with it without drinking or using.

Research shows that urges will become less frequent and intense with time. But even if they don't go away completely, with the right skills under your belt, you can manage them effectively over the long term. While you would ideally quit using drugs and alcohol after a single try and never turn back, you have probably learned through your own experience that managing urges to drink or use is not something that you can learn overnight. That is why you need a range of skills and tools to enable you to preserve your recovery anytime a situation, person, stressor, or state of mind places your recovery in jeopardy.

Who This Book Can Help

This book was written for anyone who suffers from alcohol or drug addiction. *Addiction* is an illness that involves progressively losing control over your use. When you lose control of alcohol or drug use, devastating things begin to happen as a result, but you find yourself continuing to drink or use drugs anyway. Whether or not you have been formally diagnosed with an addiction, if you feel that you have lost control over your drug or alcohol use and you want to do something about it, this book can be helpful to you. Specifically, the techniques you will learn from this book can help you to strengthen your motivation to change your alcohol or drug use, and equip you with the knowledge about addiction and a variety of coping skills that will enable you to do so successfully. You will also learn about different types of treatment that are effective for your addiction, so that if you decided to pursue formal treatment, you will know what to look for and expect. This workbook focuses on alcohol and drug addiction, which is in the category of substance addiction. Other behavioral addictions, or compulsive behaviors that may require treatment (such as gambling), are not addressed in this book.

If you are already working with a therapist or treatment provider for your addiction, the exercises in this workbook can be a part of your therapy. Taking an active role in your treatment by bringing in concepts you are learning through self-help can be useful in many ways. First, it can help you focus your treatment on learning the therapy skills that you find to be the most useful or that you need to work on the most. Second, you can build confidence in your ability to master the techniques, since you will be practicing them in these workbook exercises in between your therapy sessions. Third, since we'll devote a lot of time to working on motivation, and scientific studies have found that motivation predicts treatment success, you can improve your own prognosis by engaging in exercises to strengthen your motivation.

This workbook is not in any way intended to be a replacement for formal psychological or psychiatric treatment for addiction or any related health condition, but it can certainly be a tool for you to use while you are receiving treatment. Likewise, health care providers who work with patients who suffer from addiction may find this workbook helpful in suggesting exercises to increase motivation for change. It can also be an effective way to introduce cognitive behavioral relapse prevention skills, as well as mindfulness exercises for coping with uncomfortable emotions and cravings for alcohol and drugs.

Putting the Techniques into Practice

Thanks to the great scientific advances that have been made in addiction treatment over the past decade, there is now a broader range of skills and treatment approaches that can help you overcome your struggle with drug or alcohol addiction. Unlike other addiction workbooks, which typically focus on a a single therapy approach (such as cognitive behavioral therapy), this book features a range of research-based techniques drawing on three distinct yet compatible behavioral therapies to enable you to begin and sustain your recovery: (1) motivational therapy techniques, (2) cognitive behavioral therapy, and (3) mindfulness techniques.

Motivational therapy techniques will help you get on the road to recovery, commit to making changes to your drug or alcohol use, and, whenever you need to, revisit and strengthen your motivation when it naturally shifts. The recovery process, like the rest of life, has its ups and downs. Thus, it is entirely normal to have days when you see perfectly clearly why abstaining from alcohol and drug use is essential to living the life that you want, alternating with days when you question why you're going to all of this trouble to live a life of recovery. Grappling with your ambivalence is a good way to strengthen your motivation, especially when you have the therapeutic tools to consider both sides of it in an intentional and systematic way. These are the tools that you will learn about in chapter 3.

Cognitive behavioral therapy will help you understand how your thoughts (or *cognitions*) can trigger addictive behaviors, and how to recognize and change the "addictive thinking" that makes you vulnerable to relapse. And finally, mindfulness techniques will help you to curb your impulses to drink or use when you are experiencing the discomfort of a craving or another emotion that you naturally want to "get rid of."

To help you practice and get comfortable using the techniques, in part 2 of this workbook you will complete exercises that are easy, meaningful, and applicable to your daily life. If you use this book to help you through the daily challenges you encounter in your recovery, your experiences with the exercises will guide you to discover which strategies help you the most. This way, by the time you finish the book, you will have developed your own unique set of "go-to" skills. Not only will these skills help you to steer clear of alcohol and drugs, but you can use them to help you achieve life goals, strengthen your relationships, and live a healthier, happier life.

The Power of 12-Step Programs

You may be wondering how the techniques you will be learning in this book may or may not be compatible with 12-step programs. The short answer is that they are completely compatible with the 12-step model and, in fact, attending Alcoholics Anonymous (AA) or other self-help groups may even help you to exercise some of the skills you will learn (such as reaching out for social support when you're feeling tempted to drink or use drugs). Studies have shown that people who attend 12-step groups and "work a program" by getting involved, finding a sponsor, working the steps, and giving back—by speaking, making commitments to help out at meetings, sponsoring others, or in other ways—tend to do well in their recovery in the longer term (Morgenstern et al. 1997). That said, 12-step meetings are not the best fit for everyone, and there are many people who recover successfully without being involved in self-help meetings at all. In short, you can effectively acquire the skills in this book without attending meetings, but if you are involved in a 12-step program, you will find that what you learn in this book is compatible with the 12-step principles.

How to Use This Workbook

By now you probably have a good sense of some of the things you are going to learn about as you read on. These are the main goals of working your way through the chapters and exercises in this book:

- To understand how addiction has affected you psychologically and biologically, and what steps you need to take to enable your mind and body to heal

- To abstain from using alcohol or drugs

- To learn strategies that enable you to "check in" with yourself regularly about your motivation to change your addictive behaviors, and strengthen your motivation when needed

- To learn healthy cognitive and behavioral coping skills

- To develop a mindfulness practice in your daily life, as a way of both coping with your emotions and preventing you from giving in to urges to drink or use drugs

- To develop knowledge about the types of treatment (both psychological and medical) that are available to you

That may look like a long list of goals, but they are all interrelated, and you *can* achieve every one of them. It has happened for a lot of people—some of whom you will learn about when their stories are presented in this book—who have gone from feeling like their addiction was controlling and ruining their lives to achieving abstinence from alcohol and drugs and taking the control back. Regaining that control opens up a whole new world of possibilities, and many recovering addicts use this control as the core building block of a happy, meaningful life. This is not to say that it will be easy. Although each person's struggles are unique, all addicts struggle at various points in their recovery.

This struggle is part of the hand you've been dealt in your life as someone vulnerable to the disease of addiction. To overcome it successfully, you will undoubtedly experience discomfort, frustration, vulnerability, tension, and—at times—even hopelessness. The key is to keep at it and never give up. Remember, it is not uncommon for an addict to go through treatment multiple times before achieving success. Likewise, many addicts relapse multiple times before they kick the habit for good.

If you work your way through this book, chapter by chapter; take the exercises seriously (that means practice them as many times as you need to in order to feel comfortable with each new technique); and make the commitment to work *hard* at it, you will get the most you possibly can out of it. While it is suggested that you complete the chapters in part 2 in order, you should not hesitate to come back to chapter 3 any time you feel that you need to revisit your motivation for recovery.

The therapeutic skills that you will learn in part 2 of this workbook can be used alone or in combination. These techniques are designed to arm you with a range of effective tools for managing your addiction, but you will not necessarily find each of them to be equally helpful. That is okay! There is no "one-size-fits-all" approach to treating addiction. You will get the most you can out of this workbook by trying each step in order and evaluating which steps are the most helpful to you. If you have a therapist who can talk with you about each of the skills as you progress through the workbook, your therapist can help you to explore each concept as it relates to your personal, unique set of addictive behavior patterns. However, it isn't necessary—this workbook can be helpful to you regardless of whether you are in treatment. So let's get on the road to your recovery and begin this healthy new chapter of your life!

PART 1

Understanding Addictive Behaviors

CHAPTER 1

How Addiction Happens

T hink back to the first time you realized that your control over your use of alcohol or drugs was slipping away from you. Maybe someone said something about it and you felt defensive (though you probably know by now, you felt defensive because it was true!). Perhaps you recognized it yourself and tried harder to moderate your use, but you kept on coming to the same conclusion: one drink, one hit, one pill was no longer enough. One always led to more, and more led you to problems in your life. Yet even the problems weren't enough to give you the strength to stop. The urge to continue, even if it made no sense, was too strong. This is what it is to have an addiction. You lose control over your use of drugs or alcohol, wreaking havoc on your life, and you find yourself continuing to drink or use anyway.

In this chapter, we'll go into greater depth about the signs and symptoms of addiction, and you will learn about some of the things that might have made you vulnerable to addiction. After completing the exercises that help you identify your personal addiction risk factors and symptoms, should you decide that you need a professional to evaluate you, this chapter provides guidance to help you identify a qualified professional who can help.

How Is Addiction Diagnosed?

Though you can easily look in a textbook or on the Internet to find the criteria that are used to determine whether someone has an addiction, you can probably define it just as well by reflecting on your own experience. What led you to believe that you were in need of help to manage your use of alcohol or drugs, and what were the consequences of your use in your life? As you are learning, addiction usually has to do with a loss of control over drinking or using drugs. Let's think about how that might unfold. Consider what it was like when you started drinking or using. If you are like most people, you started drinking for one of three reasons:

- Alcohol or drugs made you feel really good.

- They helped you to feel better when you were not feeling well (for example, when you were in physical pain or discomfort, or when you were experiencing negative emotions such as sadness, anxiety, or anger).

- They enhanced your performance at something (for example, sports or the ability to work long hours without getting tired).

If you were seeking the good, pleasurable feelings, or the performance enhancement, then your motivation was for what is known as *positive reinforcement*. If you were trying to alleviate physical or emotional pain, then you were "self-medicating" with alcohol or drugs. (This is also called *negative reinforcement* because you are drinking or using to "take away" something unpleasant, like pain.)

Regardless of the reason you were drawn to alcohol or drugs, in the beginning, it worked. You came to expect certain physical and emotional sensations when you were drinking or using, and just like we come to expect pleasure from a tasty dessert when we eat it (and the pleasure always comes!), you knew that you could count on feeling the sensations you were expecting each time you drank alcohol or used drugs. And this is what kept the pattern going: the more these expectations of elation, relaxation, happiness, confidence, relief, or any other sensation you were seeking were fulfilled, the more you wanted to drink or use drugs.

At some point, a transition occurred. The usual sequence of *drink or use, and feel good or better* did not work in the same way that it did initially. Maybe you developed *tolerance*. This happens when the amount of alcohol or drug that first gave you the feeling you were seeking no longer works in the same way; you begin to need more. Maybe you started to experience *withdrawal symptoms*, which are the unpleasant effects of alcohol or drugs leaving your body. These symptoms can lead you to want to drink or use more so that you will feel better. Though these effects are different depending on which drug you use, they usually involve a combination of unpleasant physical sensations (such as nausea or vomiting, headaches, shaking, and sweating) and emotions (such as depression and anxiety). When the symptoms of tolerance or withdrawal begin, this often marks the progression of what started as social or recreational alcohol or drug use to problematic use. As this transition occurs, you start to feel that you need to drink or use just to feel normal.

So, how do you know when you're addicted? It's when that need—to drink or use to feel normal—starts to override most of the other things you value in life. During that process, people and things that are important in your life become affected by what has now turned into *compulsive* drug or alcohol use. This happens because, when you are so preoccupied with drinking or using to feel "okay," other things you used to do with the time that you spend using, recovering from using, and planning to use again start to fall by the wayside. What's more, despite its negative impact on one or more aspects of your life (such as your ability to be productive, your physical and emotional well-being, and your important relationships), you find yourself continuing to drink or use anyway. In the 12-step philosophy this is often referred to as the "insanity" of addiction; you keep on doing the same thing over and over again (drinking or using), yet you are expecting different results. You think, *It's not going to get out of hand this time!* when, in reality, your days of drinking or using in moderation are far behind you.

Let's take a look at how this pattern developed in Charlie's life.

Charlie's Story

Charlie is a twenty-three-year-old man who is attending a local university as a Computer Science major. He experimented with drugs and alcohol throughout his teens, with phases of smoking pot daily alternating with phases of heavy drinking. But pot and alcohol were easy for him to give up and he never considered himself to be a person with "addictive tendencies."

When he was in his second year of college, a friend of his offered to share some pills he was taking to enhance his ability to pay attention and stay up for long hours during final exams. The pills, called Adderall, were prescribed to his friend for attention deficit disorder, but his friend took a little more than he was prescribed and found that it helped him when he needed to cram for exams or big assignments. Charlie thought, *Why not?* and after trying the Adderall a few times, he found that it really enhanced his performance in school during finals. So he started asking around and found someone to supply him, just in case he wanted to get it in a crunch.

After a few months of using Adderall on and off, Charlie found himself using the pills not only for finals or major assignments, but habitually for studying or homework. Adderall became somewhat of a crutch for focusing his attention. Despite the benefits, Charlie, who was normally a very upbeat and sociable person, found himself feeling irritable, preferring to be alone much of the time. When he wanted to sleep after studying for long hours on Adderall, he just couldn't bring his energy level down and he found himself struggling with terrible insomnia. Though he tried to cut back on the Adderall several times, each time he found that his concentration was poor, and he felt stressed about the impact this could have on his grades.

In an attempt to resolve his insomnia problem, Charlie acquired a prescription for some sleeping pills, but they didn't work. He found himself doubling and sometimes tripling the dose to get to sleep. After only a few weeks of alternating between the sleeping pills and the Adderall, Charlie felt overtired and unable to think clearly. As a consequence, he was less productive at school. Charlie was becoming more and more isolated from his friends, and his grades started to slip. His life suddenly seemed to be dominated by pills: thinking about them, coming down from them, feeling the urge to take them, and planning how he was going to manage the balance between the uppers (Adderall) and the downers (sleeping pills) so that he could get everything done. Though he was trying his best to keep it all together, his life was slowly coming apart.

Though Charlie was working a part-time job at the campus bookstore, the cost of taking Adderall regularly began to add up and he started running out of money. As his supply of Adderall ran out, he felt depressed, irritable, unmotivated, and unable to concentrate. His parents came to visit him at school just prior to spring break, and without a thought, he took his mother's checkbook out of her purse and wrote himself several checks of a few hundred dollars each to cash. Maybe, he thought, if the amounts were not so large and he cashed them gradually, she wouldn't notice.

Like Charlie, you have probably found yourself acting in ways that are completely out of character for you when drugs or alcohol have taken hold of you and your life. What started out as using to feel good or to alleviate some negative feelings (or if you're like Charlie, to enhance your performance in some way) somehow got very out of hand. Much of this has to do with the effects of substances on the brain, which are explained in the next chapter. But first, let's spend a few minutes looking over the signs and symptoms of addiction.

Exercise 1.1: Addiction Signs and Symptoms

Below is a list of signs and symptoms of addiction. Place a check next to those that you have experienced in the past twelve months.

Tolerance

_____ You need to use more alcohol or drugs to feel the desired effect.

_____ The same amount of alcohol or drugs doesn't do what it used to.

Withdrawal

_____ When you don't have alcohol or drugs, you are uncomfortable physically or emotionally.

_____ You've used alcohol or another substance to help make yourself feel better when you were coming down from alcohol or drugs.

Craving

_____ You think about drugs or alcohol frequently.

_____ Until you've acted on an urge by drinking or using, it is very hard to get it out of your head.

Loss of Control

_____ You've made rules for yourself concerning how much you will drink or use but you were unable to stick to them.

_____ You've tried to quit or cut back your use of alcohol or drugs but were not able to.

_____ You've found yourself drinking or using more than you had planned to or for a longer period of time than you meant to.

_____ You've felt at times that you couldn't fit in or feel good without alcohol or drugs.

_____ You have used alcohol or drugs when you were feeling upset or angry with someone.

_____ You have blacked out (or had periods of time for which you have no memory) when under the influence of alcohol or drugs.

_____ You have overdosed on drugs.

_____ You have used one or more drugs without knowing what it was or how it would affect you.

_____ The thought of running out of drugs or alcohol makes you anxious.

Legal Problems

_____ You have been arrested or had other legal problems as a result of drinking or using.

_____ You have stolen things to pay for alcohol or drugs.

Problems in Social or Occupational Functioning

_____ You have made mistakes at work or school because of your use of drugs or alcohol.

_____ Your use of alcohol or drugs has hurt your relationships with others.

_____ You have not been able to fulfill important role obligations (such as household chores, financial responsibilities, or caring for children or other loved ones) as a result of drinking or using.

_____ You have lost interest in hobbies or things you used to enjoy (such as spending time with friends or family) while increasing the time you spend drinking or using.

Persistent Use Despite Negative Consequences

_____ Despite your awareness of one or more negative effects of alcohol or drugs on some aspect of your life or ability to function, you find yourself continuing to drink or use drugs anyway.

Impairment or Distress Resulting from Use

_____ You have not taken good care of yourself (for example, not eating well or not practicing good hygiene) because of your alcohol or drug use.

_____ Drinking or using drugs has caused or worsened existing psychological or medical problems (such as depression, anxiety, or cardiovascular disease).

If you marked any of the signs and symptoms that go beyond tolerance and withdrawal, you have, at a minimum, experienced alcohol- or drug-related problems. Some people experience such problems without actually being addicted, and they decide to quit or cut back on drinking or using. These are very healthy choices, because having had the experiences described on the checklist suggests that you may be at risk for greater problems (including addiction) if you continue to drink or use. In the Resources section you will find resources for learning about _controlled drinking_ or _harm reduction_ approaches to the use of alcohol or drugs. The goal of harm reduction is to reduce, but not quit, drinking or using. It is important for you to know, however, that this workbook is written for those who suffer from addiction and are open to an abstinence-based program of recovery.

This exercise is not intended to substitute for a formal diagnosis of addiction. It will, however, help you to reflect on the way your use of alcohol and drugs has affected your life. If you have not been evaluated professionally, your responses may provide some indication of whether it would be a good idea to find out more about the seriousness of your problem and consider treatment that extends beyond self-help.

If you think that you may have an addiction, but you are not sure, then you should be evaluated by a professional right away. Ideally you should seek out a professional with expertise in addiction. Appropriate professionals may include medical doctors, psychologists, counselors or therapists (with a master's degree in either psychology or social work), or admissions counselors at addiction treatment facilities.

How and Where to Seek Professional Help

Finding the appropriate professional to conduct a careful evaluation of your addiction symptoms is not always easy, especially if this is a new problem or if you have never seen a professional to help you with mental or emotional problems. If you have seen a mental or behavioral health professional in the past or are currently working with someone whom you trust, even if that person has not helped you previously with problems related to your alcohol or drug use, it is a good idea to share your concerns with that person, and ask them (1) if they have training and experience that will enable them to assess or treat you for this type of problem, and (2) if not, whether they can recommend an addiction expert whom you can see for an evaluation. If you don't have a mental health professional to work with but you have a primary care doctor with whom you feel comfortable, you can request a referral to an addiction specialist from your doctor. It is always an advantage if you can get a referral from a trusted medical professional to someone else with whom they have worked. That way, the referring professional has a good sense of the quality of the person or program to which you're being referred.

Sometimes people feel hesitant to talk with their doctor or counselor about alcohol or drug use because they are worried that the information will be shared with a family member or someone else. Remember that there are very strict privacy laws that prevent doctors and other professionals from sharing anything you tell them about your alcohol or drug use with anyone else without your explicit permission (unless you share information that indicates that you may seriously harm yourself or another person).

When you talk with a doctor or other professional for the first time about your concern that you might have a drug- or alcohol-related problem, there are three key elements you can introduce to the conversation to help make it go smoothly and minimize your discomfort:

1. *Let the person know how hard it is for you to talk about this.* This will set the tone for the conversation and engage the person's feelings of empathy toward you.

2. *Describe your concerns succinctly and straight to the point, without going into detail until the person asks questions.* This will help you to get your point across clearly, and then, as you get a sense of the other person's reaction and your comfort level with the conversation, you can decide how much detail you are comfortable sharing.

3. *Make a direct request for what you hope to get out of the conversation.* If you are seeking a referral, ask for it directly. If you are concerned about your privacy and confidentiality concerning what you are revealing, express that directly and ask that the information be kept confidential.

Finding the Words

Let's take a look at how Charlie expressed the need for professional help, using the three key conversation elements described above. Even though Charlie felt that he couldn't help himself when he stole the checks from his mother, he struggled with intense guilt and shame afterward, and he began to recognize that he was losing control over his behaviors surrounding his use of Adderall. Even though part of him didn't want to give up Adderall, perhaps a greater part of him realized that he was acting in ways that were concerning and that he needed professional help.

Charlie had a pediatrician whom he really felt he could trust. His pediatrician treated him for general health issues all the way up until he went away to college, and even though he felt self-conscious about approaching him to talk about the problems he was having with Adderall, he didn't feel ready to talk with his parents about it. He knew, however, that it was only a matter of time before his mom would notice the checks he had stolen from her and that, sooner or later, the truth would come out. Charlie realized that if he needed to tell his mom about his drug problems, he would be better off doing that with the advice of a professional. So he called his pediatrician, Dr. Amira.

Charlie: Hi, Dr. Amira. Thank you for taking the time to talk with me.

Dr. Amira: You're welcome, Charlie. What's going on?

Charlie: Well, this is very difficult for me to talk about because I feel worried for myself and, at the same time, very ashamed about this problem that I am having. So please bear with me.

Dr. Amira: Okay.

Charlie: Before I tell you about the problems I've been having, I need to ask you about the confidentiality of the things that I tell you. Are you able to talk with me about some issues I'm having without sharing what I say with my family?

Dr. Amira: Yes, Charlie. Everything you say to me is completely confidential, unless you tell me something concerning about your safety or the safety of someone else, such as expressing an intention to harm yourself or another person. Or if you tell me about someone who is being abused—under those circumstances I would need to report what you tell me to protect you or someone else who is in danger. But anything else that you say to me will stay between us.

Charlie: Thank you. It helps to know that. The reason I called is because you are the only person I trust to tell about what has been going on with me. I started using Adderall to stay up and study for finals, and I'm concerned that I may have become addicted to it.

Dr. Amira: Yes, Adderall can be highly addictive. Let me be sure I understand you, though. Did anyone prescribe it to you, or were you getting it some other way?

Charlie: *(pausing, a little bit hesitant and embarrassed)* Well, I feel bad admitting this, but I got it from a friend at first. Nobody is prescribing it to me. The reason I was calling is because I think I need a professional to evaluate me and help steer me in the right direction, and I was hoping that you might know of an addiction specialist in the New York City area whom you could recommend.

———————————

The three key elements in the sample dialogue—all of which emphasize directness and encourage empathy—can help you not only when you are asking a professional for a referral, but also when you're communicating with friends and family about your participation in addiction treatment. We will come back to communication skills and rehearse them later, in chapter 4.

Returning to the issue of finding a competent professional to evaluate you, if you don't have a doctor or other treatment provider whom you can ask for a referral, you have a few other options. First, if you'd like to speak with a doctor who has specialized training in addiction, there are a number of professional organizations you can go through. See the Resources chapter at the end of this workbook for some examples.

Apart from individual providers such as physicians or therapists, addiction treatment programs are staffed with various qualified professionals who can evaluate your symptoms. It may be reassuring to remind yourself that making an appointment for an evaluation doesn't mean that you are committing to entering treatment. The Resources section at the end of this workbook contains some links to useful search engines for treatment programs.

Browsing the options on these websites, while very informative, can also be overwhelming if you don't know what you're looking for. There are certain questions that you will want to ask when you're looking for a treatment program, to get a sense of the quality of the program and whether it can meet your individual needs. Some examples of key questions to ask, and the responses you'd look for in a quality program, are provided in the following table.

Questions to Ask When Seeking Treatment

Question	Desired Responses
Is the treatment approach you use supported by scientific studies?	Behavioral therapies and medications are the most well studied approaches. A combination of the two is ideal.
Can you describe the types of behavioral therapies you use in your program?	The behavioral therapies with the most scientific support include cognitive behavioral therapy, motivational interviewing, and motivational incentives.
Do you provide medicines to treat addiction symptoms directly?	Medications can be prescribed to help a person to stop abusing alcohol or drugs, or to prevent relapse. Whether they are prescribed will depend on the program. Examples of medications a treatment provider might mention are naltrexone, vivitrol (an injectable form of naltrexone), acamprosate, methadone, or suboxone (also known as buprenorphine).
What range of services do you offer to tailor the plan of treatment to my individual needs?	In addition to drug abuse treatment, ideally the program will provide other services to address your unique individual needs. These may include psychiatric assessment and treatment for other conditions (such as depression or anxiety), medical treatment (including medical detoxification from drugs or alcohol if needed), family therapy, vocational programs to assist with returning to work or seeking employment after treatment is complete, self-help groups, and social services.

What type of continuing care is provided after I finish the treatment program?	Since ongoing management of your addiction is crucial for treatment success, many programs offer a continuing care or aftercare therapy group in which you can continue to receive support after you have "graduated" from the program. Inquire about therapy or supportive groups you can participate in once you've completed treatment. If none are provided, then you'll want to discuss how ongoing care plans will be developed for longer-term management of your addiction after you finish treatment.
Is drug or alcohol use monitoring included in the program?	To be sure that your individual needs are being met, ongoing drug testing should be part of your care, so that if you relapse during treatment, your treatment plan can be adjusted accordingly to maximize your chances of treatment success. A healthy treatment philosophy is that relapse does not indicate failure; it means that the treatment plan needs to be revisited and individualized to address the specific problems that are being encountered.
How long is treatment?	Research studies show that at least three months of treatment is usually needed to effectively help you to stop using alcohol or drugs and maintain your treatment benefits. Studies generally show that the longer a person stays in some form of treatment, the better.
Is 12-step self-help part of the program?	The social support from 12-step groups can be helpful both during and after treatment has ended. Ideally, getting you engaged in a 12-step program will be part of your treatment.

What Makes You Vulnerable

Why me? you might find yourself asking. Why is it that some people can take or leave alcohol or drugs, experiment with them (even heavily), and then just turn the page as though it never happened? You can probably think of at least a handful of people like this whom you've known or even used to drink or use with. Now they just drink or smoke pot here and there, socially. Maybe they even get a little too drunk or high from time to time, but for the most part, they keep it under control.

Why can't I do that? you may wonder. Many people who seek out help for their alcohol or drug use find themselves, at some point in the process, wishing they could be that person who could take it or leave it. You might find yourself fantasizing about drinking or using socially at some point, and it is normal to want to be able to do that. The loss of control over drinking or using drugs that you've experienced is *not* normal, and addressing that effectively might mean giving up your "ideal" of drinking or using in moderation, at least for now. It doesn't mean that for everybody, but clearly the least risky path to long-term recovery from addiction is to quit using altogether. Coming to terms with the reality of that can be very hard.

Although there is no single reason that can explain why you are more vulnerable than some of your friends or family members, studies have shown that there are common risk factors that increase the likelihood that a person will develop an addiction. The worksheet below will help you to identify some of your personal risk factors.

Exercise 1.2: Personal Risk Factors

Below you will find a list of biological, environmental, and other conditions that increase the risk for addiction. Place a check mark beside those conditions that you have experienced.

_____   You have at least one family member who suffers from addiction.

_____   You have had depression, anxiety, post-traumatic stress disorder, or other psychological problems.

_____   Your parents or other role models used alcohol or drugs excessively around you when you were growing up.

_____ Your parents or other role models engaged in criminal behavior consistently when you were growing up.

_____ You had friends and acquaintances at school who were using drugs and alcohol when you were in your teens.

_____ You had trouble in school as a child (for example, a learning disability or poor grades).

_____ You had difficulty making or keeping friends or feeling like you "fit in" with your peers when you were growing up.

_____ There was a lot of chaos and conflict at home when you were growing up (for example, lots of fighting between the adults in your home).

_____ You were physically or sexually abused.

_____ You started experimenting with alcohol or drugs as a child or in your early teen years.

_____ You have smoked or injected drugs.

_____ You had some traumatic experiences in your life prior to starting to use alcohol or drugs excessively.

The more risk factors you have, the more vulnerable you are, so if you have lots of check marks above, it will help you to make sense of why you've been affected by addiction. But even if you didn't check off anything on the list, or if you checked off only one or two risk factors, you can still develop drug or alcohol addiction.

How could that be? you might wonder. For starters, it is important to remember that these risk factors do not each have an equal influence on whether or not you become addicted. For example, genetic factors (such as whether or not you have an immediate family member with addiction) explain between 40 and 60 percent of a person's vulnerability to addiction (Kendler et al. 2000; Tsuang et al. 1998; Tsuang, Stone, & Faraone 2001). Although many people with family members who suffer from addiction do not themselves become addicted, among those who do develop an addiction, the genetic vulnerability is usually paired with conditions in the environment that "activate" problem drinking or drug use (Enoch 2012).

For example, when a person who is genetically vulnerable grows up in a chaotic home environment, where he or she is abused and witnesses a parent or role model abusing alcohol or drugs, these conditions can "activate" the genetic tendency to drink or use drugs excessively. Even with a perfectly healthy home environment, a person who suffers from depression or anxiety and is exposed to a peer group that is using drugs or alcohol would be more likely to develop an addiction than a person who experienced either one of these conditions alone.

Wrap-up

In this chapter, you've learned some important things about yourself. You explored some of the unique aspects of your history, family, and life experiences that placed you at risk for addiction. You also identified your symptoms of addiction. You can reflect on this list any time you need to strengthen or remind yourself of your motivation to keep on actively working on your recovery.

If you aren't in treatment already, you now have some guidance about how to ask health care professionals whom you know and trust to help you identify one or more treatment providers with specialty training in addiction. You can also access some helpful resources at the end of this workbook to enable you to do some research on treatment on your own, and you are armed with good questions that will help you to find the treatment program that is the best fit for you. In the next chapter, you will deepen your understanding of the way addiction has affected you biologically and how some of the effects of these substances on the brain can explain your loss of control over alcohol and drugs.

CHAPTER 2

Addiction Is a
Brain Disease

At the beginning of this book, you read about how the brain's ability to "put on the brakes" and control impulses malfunctions when you become addicted to something. As a result, you get stuck in *go* mode even when giving in to your impulses can be harmful to you. In this chapter, you will learn more about how excessive alcohol and drug use alters the brain, and how science-based medication and psychological treatments for addiction can help the brain heal in recovery. You will also become familiarized with some of the medications that are available to promote this healing process.

As you hopefully have started to process by now, you have a disease, and it is serious. The bad news is that this disease can be very destructive and not only ruins but also takes lives every single day. The good news is that it is very treatable. People can and do get better, and you can be one of them. In this workbook, you are going to learn the most effective behavioral therapy techniques that are used in addiction treatment. By practicing the combination of these strategies that are uniquely helpful to you personally, you can increase your chances of getting better. Let's take a look at how addiction affects the brain, and what you can do to help yourself heal.

The Mind on Drugs Is Not Rational

Though the stigma that follows the illness of addiction is far from gone, advances in medicine and science have deepened society's understanding of addiction as a chronic disease. As the word has spread about this in the popular media, and more celebrity faces have either come forward or tragically lost their lives to addiction, the growing curiosity about addiction has provided an opportunity to educate the public about the seriousness of the illness.

In this process, addiction experts in the media have at least partially debunked some of the myths about addiction being a "moral failing" or a "choice." Even though the initial decision to drink or use drugs is made by voluntary choice, research has shown that as alcohol or drug use progresses to addiction, the ability to make rational choices becomes affected (NIDA 2010). Because the ability to choose rationally is what enables us to choose healthy behaviors, take care of ourselves, and act as moral and ethical human beings, the impact of excessive drug use on the brain can be dangerous and disabling. As drug use becomes compulsive, the "choice" to use is not made in the rational way that we make most other choices in life.

Most of the choices we make involve weighing the pros and cons of doing one thing versus another. For example, let's take a look at the thought process of someone who has never been addicted to alcohol or drugs. Jody gets invited to a party by some friends from work. The party happens to be the day before she has an important meeting that she will need to prepare for. She goes to the party and her friends are drinking and smoking pot. In deciding whether or not she is going to drink and smoke, a lot of thoughts go through her mind—thoughts such as *If I smoke and drink with my friends, this is going to be a lot more fun*, and *I don't want to come across like a party pooper*. As she tries to figure out a solution, she has thoughts such as *Maybe I can party with my friends on another night*, and *If I don't perform well at the meeting, how will that affect me?*

Though the decision-making process may appear simple, the thoughts that run through Jody's mind reflect a complex process of reasoning and judgment that enable her to plan what to do next. Maybe the plan will be to stay a short time at the party so that she will not be overly tempted. Maybe the plan will be to have just one drink and skip smoking pot this time. This is the process that a "rational brain" goes through to arrive at a decision. Whether or not the decision turns out to be the best one, it comes at the end of a rational thought process.

When you are addicted to something, that rational process becomes impaired; your actions in relation to using drugs and alcohol become dominated by your impulses, while the part of your brain that controls reasoning, judgment, and weighing pros and cons malfunctions. Here's why:

How Drugs Act in the Brain

From the time we're born, our brains are wired to reward pleasurable experiences. For example, when we eat something that tastes delicious or when we hear music that we enjoy, our brain's reward system releases brain chemicals that produce feelings of pleasure. These brain chemicals (also known as neurotransmitters) are part of the brain's communication system. The nerve cells in your brain release these chemicals, which act as "messengers." They carry messages between nerve cells. When you eat something delicious, a nerve cell releases a neurotransmitter called dopamine. This nerve cell is the one that is "sending" the message. The message has to be received for you to experience pleasure. What happens next is the dopamine attaches to another "receiving" nerve cell. Once the message has been received, any "extra" dopamine that remains in the space between the two cells (known as the synapse) is recycled or brought back into the "sending" nerve cell.

What do you feel when all of these messages are going back and forth in the nerve cells in your brain? When it involves the release of dopamine, the brain's natural pleasure chemical, you feel great, and you want to repeat the behavior. Alcohol and most drugs that people become addicted to interfere with the brain's communication system. Their chemical structure is so similar to some of our natural brain chemicals, like dopamine, that they can convey a "false" message to a nerve cell, causing it to release unusually large amounts of dopamine. They can also prevent extra dopamine from being recycled, so that it continues to send messages to other nerve cells. Dopamine starts flooding the brain's reward system, and the system becomes overstimulated. When triggered by alcohol or another drug, the brain releases two to ten times more dopamine than it does when you eat something delicious or have another natural and pleasurable experience like listening to music or having sex (Di Chiara and Imperato 1988). The exaggerated sense of pleasure, or *euphoria*, that you experience when this happens leads to an intense desire to repeat the experience.

Our natural pleasure response involving dopamine was designed to promote survival. The experience of pleasure that we get from eating, intimacy, and other enjoyable activities is the reason that we repeat these acts. These acts are vital; without food and human contact we cannot stay healthy or live for very long. But the pleasure response that is triggered by repeated alcohol and drug use has the opposite effect—rather than promoting survival and well being, it causes emotional and physical suffering, a *diminished* ability to experience pleasure, and a *diminished* ability to carry out life-sustaining activities (such as working, eating, and taking care of yourself), while at the same time compelling a person to continue to drink or use.

As destructive as this cycle is, biologically it actually makes sense. Here's what happens: with repeated drug or alcohol use, the brain's production of dopamine becomes depleted, and with less dopamine available in the brain, using alcohol or drugs just doesn't work as well to produce that intense euphoria or high. And neither does anything else, for that matter. When we don't have enough dopamine in our brains, the things that used to bring us pleasure just don't do the trick anymore; this loss of pleasure can lead to depression, hopelessness, and a lack of interest in the things that we once enjoyed.

When people are in this predicament, not only do they feel the need to drink or use drugs to try and bring their dopamine back to the way it used to be, but they need to use larger amounts of alcohol and drugs to trigger that same dopamine rush they experienced back when all of this started. This is known as tolerance. You may recall from chapter 1 that tolerance is one of the warning signs that a person is at risk of transitioning from social use of alcohol or drugs to addiction. You may also have heard the popular expression "chasing that first high." That's when you keep on trying, in vain, after becoming addicted to something, to get back to a high that is just like the first one you ever had on it. As you are now learning, the trouble is, once you build up tolerance, you just don't have enough dopamine to get to that place anymore. That is why, when you cross that threshold and become addicted, the "chase" can never be satisfied.

In the longer term, addiction leads to other brain changes that make it hard to give up your use of alcohol and drugs. The parts of your brain that work together to enable you to control and plan rational behavior, such as the frontal lobe, can be damaged by excessive alcohol or drug use. At the same time, brain chemicals that influence your ability to learn can become depleted, causing problems with your ability to think and reason. When this happens, seeking out ways to get and use alcohol or drugs can come to resemble a habit that a person repeats without even realizing it. It becomes like a reflex, something you do automatically without thinking—especially when you're in a place or with a person you associate with drinking or using. In fact, understanding how people, places, and things can be *associated* with drinking or using is going to be a very important part of overcoming your addiction.

How Addictive Behavior Is Learned

If you know a little bit about psychology, you have probably heard of Pavlov and his scientific experiments. Pavlov was interested in learned behavior, especially a process called *associative learning*, in which a pair of stimuli or experiences can become associated with one another. In his famous experiment using his dog, Pavlov found that if he rang a bell just before feeding his dog, and he did this over and over again, his dog could learn to anticipate or *expect* that the food was coming just upon hearing the bell ring. This became apparent to Pavlov when the dog began salivating every time he heard the bell, even before he could see or taste any food. The learned association between the sound of the bell and the experience of eating was so strong that the dog developed what is called a *conditioned response* to the bell. Salivating is a conditioned response that is designed to prepare the body to eat.

In the same way that Pavlov's dog learned that the bell was a *cue* that signaled that food was coming, people can "learn" addictive behaviors. When you drink or use drugs frequently around certain people or in certain places, you learn to associate those people or places with the experience of being high or intoxicated. People and places become "cues" just like the bell in Pavlov's experiments. These cues create an anticipation of drinking or using drugs and all of the feelings that go along with being intoxicated or high. That anticipation can create an intense urge or craving.

Emotions can become cues as well; when you drink or use drugs repeatedly when you are in a certain emotional state (for example, when you are angry, sad, or nervous), then the emotional state itself can become a conditioned cue. For these reasons, being around people, places, or things (such as emotions) that remind you of drinking or using can trigger powerful cravings that are so uncomfortable that drinking or using seems like the only choice. These cravings are your *conditioned response* to drug and alcohol cues.

Retraining the Brain

When Pavlov's dog salivated in response to the bell, it was like a reflex. When addiction takes hold, your reactions to alcohol or drug cues can become very automatic, much like reflexes. Our most basic reflexes are controlled by the lower, more primitive part of our brains, including the brainstem. Can you recall a time when you found yourself drinking or using and you couldn't recall how you even decided or started to drink or use? If so, that is because the addicted part of your brain was driving your behavior.

We will continue to refer to your *addicted brain* throughout this workbook; this is the part of your brain that will tempt and drive you to fulfill your impulses. These impulses make you feel like you "need" to drink or use, especially when you encounter cues that trigger cravings. To overcome your addiction, you will need to learn to purposely retrain the more sophisticated, rational part of your brain, which involves your frontal lobe. As you work your way through the exercises in this book, this is exactly what you are going to learn to do!

We will also refer to your *rational brain* throughout the workbook, to highlight the ways in which the addicted and rational parts of your neurobiology will conflict, and help you train your rational brain to become stronger. The frontal lobe controls rational behaviors. These behaviors are the outcome of a decision process, the kind that involves considering the pros and cons of your actions and choosing between alternatives—just as Jody did when she had to decide whether to drink and smoke pot the night before an important meeting.

When you learn to use your rational brain to make decisions about drinking or using in recovery, you will tune in to your cravings so that you realize what is happening in your body and mind in that moment, have an internal dialogue about it, and then *choose how to respond* to it, rather than *reacting to it automatically*, like a reflex. Because of the way your brain has been affected by drug or alcohol use, your automatic, reflexive reaction will be to drink or use drugs in many situations. Learning to control that reflex is what recovery is all about. You will learn how to do this in chapters 3 through 10.

The following table summarizes some of the brain structures and chemicals that are affected by addiction, and how these brain changes influence behavior.

Brain Effects of Drugs and Alcohol: How They Affect Behavior

Brain Structure/Chemical That is Affected	Result of Brain Changes (Addictive Behavior)
Dopamine is released in abnormally large amounts.	Experience of euphoria, leading to strong motivation to repeat drug use.
Dopamine production is reduced overall (with repeated substance use).	Loss of ability to experience pleasure from drugs or other activities that used to be enjoyable.
Glutamate (a brain chemical that influences our ability to learn) concentration is altered.	Loss of cognitive abilities (including effects on memory, concentration, ability to understand information and think rationally).
Frontal lobe changes.	Compromised ability to resist impulses and make planned, rational choices about behavior.
Changes in Hypothalamic-Pituitary-Adrenal Axis (part of the body's stress response system).	Compromised ability to cope with stress, leading to intensified anxiety or discomfort. Increased likelihood of drinking or using in the face of stress, as it becomes more difficult to plan or select a healthy coping response.

How Treatment Works

You might be wondering, *If addiction is a brain disease, then how exactly does treatment fix that?* Just as much of your addictive behavior has been learned, recovery-oriented behaviors are also learned. You can't erase your brain's memories of using drugs and alcohol in response to various conditioned cues—whether those cues are people, places, or things. Those cues will probably make you uncomfortable by triggering cravings for a while. But you *can* learn new responses to those cues, while you give your brain the time it needs to heal. The longer you are able to remain abstinent from alcohol or drugs, the greater your chances of successfully living without drinking or using in the long term. In part 2 of this workbook, you will learn three sets of therapeutic skills to help you achieve abstinence from alcohol or drugs: cognitive behavioral therapy, motivational techniques, and mindfulness strategies.

Cognitive behavioral therapy (CBT). CBT is a therapy approach that has been used very effectively to help people with a wide range of problems, including addictions of all kinds, mood and anxiety disorders, weight control, chronic pain management, and other mental and physical health conditions. When applied to changing addictive behaviors, CBT is also referred to as relapse prevention therapy. The techniques offered by CBT are based on the understanding of addictive behaviors as learned, conditioned responses to people, places, and things that have been associated with drinking and using. The goals of CBT are to help you (1) understand how your addictive behaviors were learned and conditioned; (2) identify the people, places, and things that have been conditioned to bring on cravings to use substances (in other words, your triggers); and (3) learn healthy coping responses to these triggers that enable you to remain abstinent from drug or alcohol use.

CBT is probably the most well studied form of psychotherapy for addictions. There have been literally dozens of clinical trials comparing CBT to other forms of addiction treatment, and the results consistently show that this approach effectively reduces drug and alcohol use for people with various types of addictions, including stimulant (Rawson et al. 2004), marijuana (Budney et al. 2006), alcohol (Annis and Davis 1989), and opioid addictions (Church et al 2001; McAuliffe 1990; Pollack et al. 2002; Stein et al. 2004).

Motivational techniques. If you're like most people in recovery, since the day you first realized that you needed to do something about your addiction, your intention to quit drinking or using has been at times clear and strong, while at other times less certain, or even completely absent. This could vary from day to day, or even from hour to hour. It is simply a reflection of the ambivalence, or mixed feelings, that all of us have when we are going to make a difficult change. Motivational therapy techniques help you to figure out the source of your ambivalence and resolve it so that you can move your life forward and commit firmly to making changes (Miller, 1983).

Motivational therapy techniques help you to explore your own ideas about how recovery could change your life, so that you can come to your own conclusions about it and become the driver of your recovery plan. Studies show that this approach is helpful for motivating people with addictions to attend therapy (Hettema, Steele, and Miller 2005), and when you combine motivational techniques with CBT, they are especially useful for helping you to quit using alcohol and drugs (Glasner-Edwards et al. 2013; Rohsenow et al. 2004). In chapter 3, you will complete motivational exercises to help you resolve ambivalence you might have about quitting drinking or using, and strengthen your commitment to your recovery.

Mindfulness-based relapse prevention. Mindfulness, one of the most well-studied forms of meditation practice, is a tool that has been recently introduced to the world of addiction treatment. Originally part of Buddhist meditation practice, mindfulness was adapted more than thirty years ago for use in a stress reduction program that was developed by Jon Kabat-Zinn (1982). Since that time, mindfulness has been used effectively to help with a range of psychological problems, including depression, anxiety, grief, and stress in individuals with serious medical problems. Mindfulness meditation, which you will learn about and practice in chapter 7, focuses on two core skills that can help you in your recovery: (1) learning how to be present in the moment, using awareness of your breath as a tool; and (2) learning to accept your experience just as it is, without judging yourself for it or trying to change it. As you will learn in chapter 7, these skills can be helpful to get you through a craving or to cope with another unpleasant emotion without turning to alcohol or drugs.

Medications

Medication is an option in the treatment of alcohol and certain drug addictions; and for some (for example, opioid addiction), it's crucial, as highlighted by a recent quote in *Time* magazine by one of the leaders in the field of drug addiction treatment,

Dr. Richard Rawson. Discussing use of the medication buprenorphine (which you will learn more about below) as a means of preventing opioid overdose deaths, which have increased in recent years, Rawson states, "Failure to encourage patients to use these medications is unconscionable. It's comparable to conducting coronary bypass surgery and failing to prescribe aspirin, lipid, and blood pressure medications as part of a discharge plan" (*Time*, Feb 2, 2014).

Combining medication with behavioral therapy techniques can be a very effective way of treating addiction. The techniques in this workbook are compatible with the use of medication, which may also help you to achieve a long enough period of time without relapsing that you can engage more fully in the psychological skills–building process. Most of the medications for addictions work in one of three ways: (1) by minimizing the intense cravings that often stand in the way of successfully quitting drug or alcohol use; (2) by blocking or preventing the "high" or "rush" that you experience when you use alcohol or drugs, making substance use less appealing; or (3) by substituting for or "replacing" the drug that you are addicted to, keeping a steady level of a similar chemical in the system. Although historically the idea of using a medication or "drug" to treat a "drug problem" has been controversial, as addiction has become better understood as a chronic illness requiring ongoing treatment, much like diabetes and heart disease (McLellan et al. 2000), medications for addiction have been demonstrated scientifically to save lives, reduce deaths by overdose, improve overall quality of life, and enable people with addictions to flourish as productive members of society.

The table that follows summarizes the available medications that are approved by the Food and Drug Administration (FDA) and currently used, most successfully in combination with behavioral therapies. There are a few additional medications that are not FDA-approved but have been studied in clinical trials and show promise for the treatment of addictions; these include Topamax, Zofran, Seroquel, and baclofen. For more information on medications that can be used to treat addiction, you can visit the website of the National Institute on Drug Abuse: http://www.drugabuse.gov.

FDA-Approved Medications Used to Treat Addiction

Medication	How It Works
Naltrexone	Treats alcohol and opioid addictions. Available in a form that can be taken orally (Revia) or by injection (Vivitrol). Blocks the pleasurable feelings if a person drinks or takes opioids while on it. Reduces cravings.
Acamprosate	Used to treat alcoholism. Available in oral form (Campral). Reduces alcohol cravings.
Disulfiram	Used to treat alcoholism. Available in oral form. Makes the person feel ill if alcohol is consumed.
Methadone	Treats opioid addiction. Available in oral and injectable forms. Used for opioid detoxification and to prevent relapses. Reduces withdrawal symptoms and cravings.
Buprenorphine	Treats opioid addiction. Available in oral/sublingual (under the tongue) form. Used for opioid detoxification and to prevent relapses. Reduces cravings and blocks the euphoria, or pleasurable feelings, if a person uses opioids.

The Brain Heals; So Do You

As strong as the evidence is that addiction has damaging effects on the brain, scientific studies have shown that the brain has a remarkable potential for recovery. In one study, using brain imaging techniques, the researchers studied images of the brains of people who were addicted to methamphetamine, looking at changes in the images repeatedly over fourteen months of recovery and comparing them to healthy individuals who had never used drugs. They found that, over time, the brain's potential to make dopamine, which was quite compromised at the beginning of the study, gradually recovered among those who remained abstinent from drugs (Volkow et al. 2001).

Even more recently, a group of scientists completed a similar brain imaging study, except that this study was designed to find out whether behavioral therapy for addiction could produce changes in brain activity in areas of the brain that are thought to be damaged by addiction. The researchers found that individuals who received cognitive behavioral therapy to treat their addictions showed improvement from the start to end of treatment on a test of impulse control and other cognitive abilities. They also showed changes in brain areas that control rational decision-making and "self-control," or the ability to control your responses to your impulses (DeVito et al. 2012).

What does this mean for me? you might be wondering. It means that, with the right therapeutic skills in place, such as those you will learn in this workbook, not only can you learn to control your behavior as it relates to drug and alcohol use, and recover your ability to make healthy decisions, but you can experience pleasure again from ordinary, naturally enjoyable experiences. When drugs and alcohol take hold and you lose control, it is easy to feel hopeless, especially when the depression sets in. The great news about these scientific studies is that they show that your life can return to normal if you receive treatment using the techniques we are focusing on in this workbook, and are able to remain abstinent from drugs and alcohol.

Wrap-up

By now, you have a deeper understanding of how addiction affects the brain. Many of your addictive behaviors can be explained by the neurobiological changes you have endured from your drug or alcohol use. In this chapter, you learned how rational decision-making is affected by chronic drinking and drug use. We reviewed how addictive behaviors are learned, and how they can become automatic. The therapy techniques you will learn in the chapters that follow can help you to learn new responses to the cues that previously triggered alcohol or drug use. By "relearning" how to respond to these cues in a healthy way without drinking or using, you are strengthening your rational brain, while disengaging from your addicted brain. This will allow you to heal and rebuild your ability to make rational choices. In the next chapter, we will begin working on strengthening your motivation for recovery.

PART 2

Overcoming Addictive Behaviors

CHAPTER 3

Step 1: Strengthen Your Motivation and Commit to Change

Have you ever wondered why it is that you can feel entirely convinced one day that drinking or using is something that has become toxic in your life, yet the next day, or even the next hour, you can find yourself coming up with reasons why it might be okay to drink or use just one more time? Believe it or not, there are theories in psychology about why this happens, because in reality, it happens to a lot of people—and not just people who are trying to quit using drugs and alcohol. This shift in motivation is something that people experience when they're trying to make all sorts of life changes, whether it's trying to eliminate a behavior that is not good for them (like overeating or overspending) or starting something new and healthy (like exercising, taking medications regularly, or eating right).

In this chapter, you are going to learn about why your motivation to change important behaviors might shift around from day to day, or over longer periods of time. You will be introduced to a theory of behavior change that explains the different stages of motivation to change your use of alcohol or drugs, and how these changes influence your recovery. Next, you will do a self-assessment to get a sense of where you are in your motivation and commitment to changing your drug and alcohol use, and you'll complete exercises that help you to strengthen and sustain your motivation. You can revisit these exercises anytime you feel that you need a little psychological "boost" to remind you of why you are going to all of this trouble to cut back or quit.

How We Change

Psychologists have spent decades trying to understand the process of behavior change. What has to happen inside of our minds to motivate us to change behaviors that have been habits for a very long time? One of the most well-studied theories about this is called the transtheoretical model of behavior change (Miller 1996). In the addiction treatment field, this model has been widely used to understand and improve motivation for recovery. According to this theory, there are five different stages of motivation for change, involving thinking about, planning, starting, and sustaining behavior changes. No matter where you are in the cycle, you can move back and forth between the stages, and every person moves through the stages and changes at a different pace. Let's take a look at the different stages:

- **Precontemplation:** The first stage in the cycle is called *precontemplation*. This is the stage when you're not even really aware that you need to make any changes to your behavior. Maybe others around you have taken notice of your alcohol or drug use and are talking to you about their concerns, but it hasn't registered for you personally. Since you've picked up this workbook, you are more than likely beyond this stage, but you can probably remember a time when you felt a little burdened and maybe even defensive about other people's concerns regarding your use of drugs and alcohol, because you didn't share them. That was when you were in the precontemplation stage.

- **Contemplation:** The second stage is just what it sounds like—it is when you're starting to think about the possibility of changing. The themes that would be going around in your head in this stage are *maybe I need to make some changes*, or *maybe drinking isn't good for me anymore*, or *maybe I can't control my drug use anymore*. At this stage, you're starting to realize that your current behavior patterns are not matching up with the way you want your life to be.

- **Preparation:** When you enter the third stage, you are convinced that you need to change your behavior and you begin planning for it. This would be the stage when you start exploring ways that you can get help with your alcohol or drug use. Some signs that you are in the preparation stage could include:

- Making an appointment to see an addiction specialist

- Considering different treatment options for your addiction

- Setting a date for when you are going to quit drinking or using

- Reading through this book and planning to start the exercises

- **Action:** When you enter the *action* stage, you have initiated the plans you made during the preparation stage. This could mean that you have started treatment, are working your way through the exercises in this book, have started to go to mutual self-help groups (such as 12-step meetings), or have already cut back or quit your use of alcohol or drugs.

- **Maintenance:** When you've been able to remain consistent in making the changes you committed to in the action stage for six months or longer, you will transition to the maintenance phase. For example, if your action stage involves quitting your use of alcohol or drugs, you would move into the maintenance stage once you've been sober for six months.

Of course, in the process of recovery from addiction, a slip or relapse can naturally interrupt your progression through this sequence of stages, but it doesn't have to put you right back at the beginning. The way that you respond to a relapse makes a huge difference in your ability to regain momentum in your recovery. If you catch yourself early, and are able to prevent a slip from turning into a full-blown relapse, you can get right back into the action phase, rather than winding back to an earlier phase and feeling "stuck" there. Throughout this section of the book, you are going to learn skills that help you to understand and move beyond a slip before it gets out of hand.

Exercise 3.1: What Stage of Change Are You In?

Review the above descriptions of the five stages of change. Circle which stage you are in with regard to your motivation to change your alcohol or drug use:

Precontemplation   Contemplation   Preparation   Action   Maintenance

Now, circle the rating that describes how motivated you are to take the necessary steps to achieve abstinence, on a scale from 0 to 10, with zero being not at all motivated and 10 being the most motivated:

| 0 | 1 | 2 | 3 | 4 | 5 | 6 | 7 | 8 | 9 | 10 |

Not Motivated   *Somewhat Motivated*   *Motivated*   *Highly Motivated*

Looking at your responses to these two items, there are a few things to keep in mind. First, if you circled *Action* or *Maintenance*, congratulations! You're well on your way to a healthier new chapter of your life. Keeping your motivation strong will be important to sustain the changes that you are already making, so be sure to complete the exercises in this chapter. If you circled *Preparation*, this chapter is an ideal place for you to solidify your reasons for initiating a change and moving into *Action*. If you circled *Precontemplation* or *Contemplation*, then it's great that you are getting educated about addiction by reading this book and considering whether making a change to your alcohol or drug use is something that you'd like to pursue further. On the rating scale, if you gave yourself less than a 5, you are probably in an early stage of change (such as precontemplation or contemplation). If you gave yourself a 5 or above, some part of you—whether it is just a small part or all of you—has already decided to take steps to change your alcohol or drug use.

Regardless of which stage of change you are in, take a look at your self-rating for motivation, and ask yourself this question: *What would it take to move me up just one more point on the scale?* If you don't know the answer to that right now, don't worry. As you consider the pros and cons of changing your alcohol or drug use, as well as the reasons why it might be worth changing, you will get a better idea of how to answer that question.

Ambivalence: It's Normal in Recovery

No matter how motivated you feel about your recovery and its importance in your life right now, it is very normal to feel *ambivalence,* or mixed feelings, about the process of changing your behavior and lifestyle (Prochaska, DiClemente, and Norcross 1992). Even though your use of alcohol or drugs has caused problems for you that have led you to think about changing, there was a reason that you started drinking or using in the first place. The reason was, it was doing something that felt good or helpful to you—whether it was making you feel positive emotions or enhancing your ability to function in some way, or removing unpleasant feelings.

It is important to acknowledge that there were some positive rewards that you got out of drinking or using back when you started, and the hope to continue to get those benefits can lead you to have mixed feelings about giving it up, *even if* you haven't experienced many positives from drinking or using for a while. Those memories are powerful, and your addicted brain will tempt you to seek out alcohol and drugs in attempts to repeat these positive experiences. As you examine your motivation for change, you will begin the process of strengthening the power of your rational brain to control your addictive behaviors.

If you're anything like most people who enter recovery, you've been using alcohol or drugs for a while, so it may be hard to imagine life without it. You might even feel like you're setting yourself up to fail, because you don't believe that you can change successfully. These anxieties are completely normal. The good news is that they are not rational! Why is that good news? Because once you recognize that your thoughts or feelings are irrational, it's easier to change them. The reality is, many people who have been drinking and using for a long time are able to give it up and turn their lives around. It's not easy, but with a solid recovery plan—which you're building with the help of this workbook—and the right support in place, it is entirely possible.

In the next section, you'll consider some of the pros and cons of continuing to drink or use versus cutting back or quitting your use of alcohol or drugs. One thing to keep in mind as you complete this exercise is that the immediate or short-term benefits of drinking and using (such as improving your mood) are often the exact opposite of the longer-term effects, which come a little bit later. These can include depression or other mood disturbances, and the inability to get important things done. Being realistic about these short- and long-term effects is important so that you can take an honest look at the full range of benefits and drawbacks that come with each possible decision (such as continuing to drink or use versus changing your use patterns).

Exercise 3.2: Resolving Your Ambivalence

The best way to resolve any mixed feelings you might have about changing your use of drugs or alcohol is to give some serious consideration to the benefits of stopping your use and weigh them against the things about drinking or using that you will miss. In this exercise, you're going to think about this in four different ways. First, you're going to think about the reasons why you drink or use—the positives. Here are a few examples of things people like about drinking or using:

- It helps with anxiety.

- It helps with relaxation.

- It provides an escape from things that are difficult to cope with.

- It can be fun.

- It breaks the ice in social situations.

Second, you're going to think about some of the negative things that happen when you drink or use. This will help motivate you to change your behavior, especially if you can keep this list in mind when you experience a craving. Here are some negative effects of drinking or drug use that you might experience:

- It causes health problems, including physical discomfort when the substance wears off, getting sick, and longer term effects of certain substances (for example, liver damage, heart disease, and oral health problems).

- It causes or worsens psychological symptoms or illness, such as anxiety and depression.

- It creates financial problems.

- It leads to relationship difficulties.

- It causes you to have difficulties meeting your obligations at work, school, or home.

Third, you'll come up with a list of the benefits of reducing or quitting. Some of the benefits that you might discover are as follows:

- Feeling better physically

- Having more predictable and stable emotions

- Becoming more productive

- Improved relationships (this happens more gradually, usually)

- Feeling better about yourself

- Saving money

Fourth, you'll spend some time thinking about the things you will miss about drinking or using. Some of the drawbacks of reducing or quitting your use of alcohol or drugs might include:

- Missing the immediate positive effects of drinking or using on your mood or your ability to do certain things

- Losing or distancing yourself from friends you like because they might tempt you to drink or use

- Feeling more limited in the range of social or work activities you can participate in comfortably

- No longer being able to lean on alcohol or drugs to cope with stress or problems

Now, complete your own matrix below of the pros and cons of reducing or quitting substance use versus continuing to drink or use drugs. Be as open and honest as you can when you make this list; the better you understand the sources of any mixed feelings you have about this, the more equipped you will be to talk yourself through them when the urge to drink or use comes up.

Benefits of Reducing or Quitting

1._____

_____

2._____

_____

3._____

_____

4._____

_____

Drawbacks of Reducing or Quitting

1. _____

_____

2. _____

_____

3. _____

_____

4. _____

_____

Benefits of Continuing to Drink or Use	Drawbacks of Continuing
1._____	1._____
_____	_____
2._____	2._____
_____	_____
3._____	3._____
_____	_____
4._____	4._____
_____	_____

To use the results of the matrix to help you in your recovery, find a place where you can jot down the drawbacks of continuing to drink or use, as well as the benefits of reducing or quitting your use. Some people like to store this in their notes on their cell phone, or even on their cell phone wallpaper for a more consistent reminder. For others, writing it down on a little index card or slip of paper and carrying it around (in a wallet or purse) can be useful. Pull out the card or look at the list on your phone any time you experience a craving, to remind yourself of what you are getting out of your recovery, as well as what you stand to lose if you slip or relapse.

Remember that your addicted brain will persuade you to drink or use by enticing you with memories of the *acute*, or short-term, positive effects of alcohol or drugs. The negatives and drawbacks of drinking and using typically come afterward. But if you start thinking about them *before* you make the decision about whether or not to drink or use, you will strengthen your rational brain and increase your chances of successfully overcoming a craving without relapsing.

Boosting Your Motivation

Earlier in this chapter, you rated your motivation to reduce or quit drinking or using. You were also thinking about what it would take to move your rating up by at least one point, to make your motivation stronger. The exercise you are going to complete next will give you some things to think about that might help you answer that question. It will involve answering some questions to help you consider more carefully the concerns that you have about your drinking or drug use, the impact of your use on your life now and in the future, and your confidence in your ability to abstain from alcohol or drugs.

First, let's look at an example.

Carrie Considers Change

Carrie has been smoking pot on a daily basis for the past eight years. In general, she's been very functional for most of that time. She's held down a few different jobs as a production assistant in the television industry, she's had a long-term relationship (which she recently ended), and she has kept up a pretty active social life. Lately she's been noticing that she has a lot of anxiety. She has found herself obsessing about past decisions (such as breaking up with her most recent boyfriend), and questioning whether they were right or wrong. She has also noticed that she's been thinking a lot about her career and wondering why she hasn't really advanced from the level of assistant to something a little higher up.

These thoughts have had a depressive effect, leading her to smoke pot more often than before. Since this cycle started, Carrie has felt less motivated to get out and do the things she normally enjoys, like socializing, exercising, and spending time with her family. She has noticed a connection between smoking pot and feeling depressed and anxious, which she wasn't aware of before. Although smoking pot helps her to detach from a lot of the things she is unhappy about, Carrie has noticed that when she smokes more heavily, she enters a period of several days of not feeling like herself. On those days, she feels sad, irritable, and extra tired, and it takes a big effort for her to focus on things she needs to do at work and at home.

Carrie goes to see a psychologist for an evaluation, and one of the themes that they discuss is the connection between her use of marijuana and the problems she has been experiencing. When she comes to the appointment, Carrie is in the contemplation stage of change concerning her use of marijuana—she is starting to put together some thoughts about how it is affecting her, but she does not yet have a plan in mind about what she is going to do about it. She rates her motivation to change her marijuana use at a 5. She is somewhat motivated, but she has some ambivalence about it, especially since she's been using pot for so long and doesn't think it has affected her in many negative ways. Carrie's psychologist suggests that she consider four aspects of her thoughts about marijuana that will help her explore her ambivalence and strengthen her motivation to make a change:

- **Recognizing Marijuana Use as a Problem:** Is it a problem or isn't it a problem? It may sound like a simple question, but when you have mixed feelings about the idea of changing your behavior, you may find yourself questioning whether your hunch (that drinking or using is the source of some, or even most, of your problems) is correct. Carrie's psychologist asks her some questions about how she has noticed marijuana causing problems for her, and what kinds of things it's interfering with. These questions lead Carrie to the following observations:

  - *It is having an effect on my mood.*

  - *It is increasing my anxiety.*

  - *It interferes with my ability to concentrate and be productive at work.*

  - *It interferes with my motivation to do things I normally love doing, like spending time with my friends and family.*

  - *I'm wondering if it might be holding me back from getting further in my career. (If I had more energy and motivation, maybe I would be more proactive.)*

- **Concern About Marijuana Use:** Often people who seek help for alcohol- or drug-related problems say that they have family members or friends who have expressed concern about their use. Though this is very important, and often sets the wheels in motion for exploring the problem further, there is nothing more powerful for motivating change than *your own* concerns about the effects of your behavior on your life. Carrie's psychologist asks her to reflect on her own worries about her marijuana use. She asks Carrie to imagine what she fears will happen if she continues to smoke pot as much as she does right now for the next year or more. In other words, what is she concerned will happen if she doesn't make any changes? Carrie expresses the following concerns:

  - *I could become more depressed and anxious.*

- *I might become very isolated.*

- *If I keep on going to work spaced out after I've been smoking pot heavily, I might start making mistakes and I could get into trouble.*

- *I could start gaining weight. I'm already exercising less, and I get hungrier when I'm smoking a lot of pot.*

- **Intention to Change:** Recognizing that you have a problem with alcohol or drugs is one thing, but translating that recognition into action is a whole other process. Getting from that point of realizing that you have a problem to committing to making a change is a big and important step. It's a process of deciding that change is needed, and that making a change can lead you to a better place in your life than where you are now. Carrie's psychologist asks her to think about why changing her marijuana use is necessary, and how her life will be different if she is able to change successfully. Carrie's responses are as follows:

  - *I need to stop smoking so that I can find out if it's the marijuana holding me back from making progress in my career.*

  - *I need to stop using marijuana so that I can be myself again—this depressed, anxious person I've become just isn't me.*

  - *If I were able to stop smoking pot, I think I would be a happier, more energetic person.*

  - *If I were able to stop smoking pot, I think I would be moving up the ladder at work.*

- **Optimism:** Do you believe that you can successfully change your use of alcohol or drugs? If you have your doubts, you are not alone. This may be one of the most challenging changes you make in your life. But studies show that if you can find reasons to believe in yourself and your ability to win this battle, you will boost your chances of succeeding (Kelly and Greene 2014). This confidence in yourself is called *self-efficacy*. To help improve Carrie's self-efficacy, her psychologist asks her to think of reasons that she can believe in her ability to succeed in her recovery. Here are the reasons she comes up with:

- *I'm a very strong person. When I'm determined to do something, I always follow through.*

- *I have a strong support system for my recovery. My friends will support me, and I have several who don't smoke pot and will be very happy to see me finally quit.*

- *I've made other difficult changes before—like when I quit smoking cigarettes—and I succeeded at those.*

After Carrie completes this exercise, she finds that she has reached a new level of self-understanding about the ways that marijuana use has been affecting her life, her concerns about the effects it could have on her in the future, the things that could change for the better if she were to change her use of marijuana, and the reasons she has to be confident that she can change her marijuana use. After reflecting on all of these things, she finds that her motivation rating has changed from a 5 to a 7.

Exercise 3.3: Motivation for Change

Now it's your turn to consider your thoughts about alcohol or drugs in the same four areas that Carrie did. This exercise will help you to explore your ambivalence about changing and express your motivation for change in your own words.

1. **Consider whether alcohol or drug use is a problem for you.**

   What kinds of problems have you had in relation to your use of alcohol or drugs? Describe them here:

   _____

   _____

   _____

   _____

How has your use of alcohol or drugs interfered with, or stopped you from, doing things you wanted to do?

_____

_____

_____

_____

2. **Think about what concerns you about your alcohol or drug use.**

Is there anything that worries you about your use? Is there anything you can imagine happening to you because of it? If so, describe your concerns here:

_____

_____

_____

_____

What, if anything, are you worried will happen if you don't cut back or stop drinking or using?

_____

_____

_____

_____

3. **Think about how changing your alcohol or drug use will affect your life.**

   What makes you think that you might need to cut back or quit your use of alcohol or drugs?

   _____

   _____

   _____

   _____

   If you change your use of alcohol or drugs successfully and things work out the way you want them to, how do you imagine your life will be different?

   _____

   _____

   _____

   _____

4. **Think about the reasons that you can believe in yourself and your ability to change.**

   What inspires you to believe that change is possible for you?

   _____

   _____

   _____

   _____

Now that you have given more thought to your motivation to change your alcohol or drug use, let's revisit the motivation rating that you completed earlier. Circle the rating that describes how motivated you are to take the necessary steps to change your alcohol or drug use on a scale from 0 to 10, with zero being not at all motivated and 10 being the most motivated:

0	1	2	3	4	5	6	7	8	9	10
Not Motivated			Somewhat Motivated			Motivated			Highly Motivated	

Did your rating change from earlier? If so, that is great news! You will find that keeping that rating as high as it can be is something you may need to work at during different stages of change—even the maintenance stage. The reason for this is that at every stage of change, those ambivalent or mixed feelings about drinking or using can (and naturally do) come up. Even when you're completely stable in your recovery, you may find yourself tempted to drink or use occasionally, and then you'll need to revisit the potential benefits and drawbacks of that choice, to take a realistic look at your motivation for sobriety.

If your motivation rating did not change from earlier in this chapter, that is perfectly okay; maybe it was high to begin with and these exercises were simply a reminder of your reasons for that. If your motivation was not so high to begin with and it did not change, then it is good that you are being honest about where you are, and you can revisit the exercises in this chapter any time you think that you might have some perspective to add to strengthen your motivation. Working with a therapist might also be helpful.

Finally, whether you moved up on the scale or not, don't hesitate to push yourself further. By asking yourself what it would take for you to increase your rating by just one more point, you can continue to strengthen your motivation. Keeping the issue of your motivation on your mental radar is a big part of making it solid and maintaining it.

Wrap-up

By now, you have a better understanding of the psychology of behavior change, the specific stage of change that you're currently in, the strength of your motivation to change your alcohol or drug use right now, and your reasons for wanting to change. This understanding is the foundation for your recovery, but it is just the first layer. Next, you need a plan for how you are going to go about establishing the support that you need to succeed in achieving your goals. You also need skills that will enable you to plan for and get through difficult situations without drinking or using.

As you move through the next six chapters of this workbook, you will learn to apply cognitive behavioral, motivational, and mindfulness-based skills to the specific types of triggers, temptations, and roadblocks you face in your recovery. By the time you finish with section 2 of this book, your personalized relapse prevention plan will be in place and you will have mastered the tools that are the most helpful to you to achieve long-term recovery.

CHAPTER 4

Step 2: Set Yourself Up to Succeed

I n the last chapter, you explored and strengthened your motivation for recovery. Now that you have clear in your mind the reasons why you want and need to change your use of alcohol or drugs, it is time to make certain adjustments in your life that will set you up for the smoothest possible road to recovery. To maximize your chances of success, you will need to be prepared for the challenges that come along in early recovery. Many of these are going to be right in front of you, in your immediate environment; they can include people, places, and things that trigger urges to drink or use. Some of these triggers will be easier for you to manage than others. This chapter will prepare you to anticipate these challenges and plan ahead for them.

You're going to learn about several different ways to be prepared for the obstacles that lie ahead: First, you'll learn about why you'll need to get things that might tempt you to use out of your home environment. You'll also learn how to be mindful of your recovery when making everyday decisions that can affect it. And you will read about the importance of introducing an exercise program into your recovery plan. Next, you'll give some thought to your social life, and ways to increase your social support for recovery. Finally, you'll learn how to enhance your current close relationships and enlist the help of your loved ones in your recovery by using assertive communication.

Get Rid of "Stuff" That Helps You Drink Or Use

As your addiction developed, you formed very powerful associations between drinking or using and the "stuff" that you used to do it. *What kind of stuff?* you might be wondering. That depends on what your preferred substance is. Let's take pot, for example. Rolling papers, bongs, and pipes are examples of the different types of things that helped you to use. Now, those things themselves, because of the strong association in your mind between them and using pot, can trigger very strong urges to get high. For someone who has just stopped smoking pot, opening a drawer and finding a pipe in it can create a powerful craving. For this reason, getting all of that stuff out of your immediate environment (your home, backpack, purse, car, or anywhere else you keep it) is one of the very first steps you will need to take to prevent a slip or a relapse. If your preferred substance is alcohol, then you might need to get your favorite wine glass or shot glass out of your home. Or if you've injected any drugs, then this would mean getting needles or syringes out of your environment. And most important of all, having your substance itself within reach is an extremely powerful trigger. So if you have leftover pot, alcohol, pills, or other substances that you are trying to quit using in your home, you'll need to get rid of those as well.

If you're like most people in early recovery, this is not exactly music to your ears. You probably have some questions about these rules, and you may have some objections. Before we address those, take a moment to think about the importance of your recovery in your life, and the reasons you listed in the last chapter for quitting. Look back at the list if you can't remember all of them off the top of your head. Think about how motivated you are to quit, and whether you are ready to take the necessary steps to do so successfully, even if they are hard at first.

Below, you'll find some very common concerns and reactions that people have to the idea of getting rid of their "stuff" (also referred to as *paraphernalia*), followed by some "recovery friendly" ways to think about these concerns.

- **Concern:** *Why do I have to get rid of all of this stuff? It has value; I hate to throw it away.*

Recovery mindset: Although it's true that all of these things cost money, think about how much continuing to drink or use will cost you, both financially and in other ways. Your priority right now is to put as many *barriers* between yourself and a relapse as you can. Having all of this stuff around makes it easy for you to drink or use on a whim. Your goal is to create more barriers. The value of your paraphernalia is nothing compared to the value of your new life in recovery.

- **Concern:** *What if somebody comes over and wants to have a drink, but I've gotten rid of all of my alcohol?*

Recovery mindset: Because drinking alcohol is socially acceptable and common, this is a common sticking point. Having alcohol around to please others is something to rethink, even though you may need some time to come to terms with the risk that this poses to you. Here's the inner dialogue to try and adopt to help you prioritize your recovery: *If having alcohol in the house makes me more vulnerable to relapse, then I can't afford to have it here. My guests will learn to accept that my place is alcohol-free. If it's really important for them to drink, we can plan a social gathering at a restaurant, where they can order a drink.*

- **Concern:** *I should be strong enough to have that stuff around me without using it.*

Recovery mindset: A lot of people in early recovery come into it with the idea that willpower is a sign of progress. But there is a saying that has been used in some of the most effective CBT-based treatments for addiction: "Be Smart, Not Strong!" (Rawson et al. 2004). What that means is, testing yourself in an attempt to prove that you have willpower or strength will place you at risk for a relapse. We know from research studies using brain imaging that being exposed to visual triggers (such as seeing paraphernalia) for as little as thirty-three milliseconds can activate the addicted part of the brain and start a craving (Childress et al. 2008). You can't always control whether you are exposed to a trigger, but whenever possible, it is better for your recovery to be *smart* and avoid it than to try to be *strong* enough to resist it, placing yourself at risk for relapse.

Exercise 4.1: Paraphernalia

Below you'll find a list of some of the things to remove from your immediate environment. Check off the ones that apply to you:

_____ Alcohol

_____ Pills

_____ Marijuana

_____ Any other drugs that you've used (even if not your preferred substance)

_____ Lighters

_____ Mirrors

_____ Ashtrays

_____ Pipes

_____ Rolling papers

_____ Bongs

_____ Needles

_____ Phone numbers (of dealers or contacts you use to find drugs)—delete from your phone

_____ Medical marijuana card

Other paraphernalia to get rid of: _____

_____

_____

_____

Now that you've identified the things to remove, you need a plan. Do you feel confident that you can get rid of these things on your own, or do you need someone to do this with you? You can turn to a loved one who is supportive of your recovery, a 12-step sponsor if you have one, or an addiction treatment provider or counselor. Make a point of not procrastinating about this; once all of those temptations are out of your way, things will begin to get a little bit easier.

Become Aware of Seemingly Irrelevant Decisions

One of the most important psychological adjustments you will make as you enter recovery is to recognize that a lot of your decisions, from now on, need to be made carefully, with your sobriety in mind. There are decisions you will make about where to go, with whom to socialize, and what kinds of things to do for fun that can have a profound effect on your recovery, even if they don't seem related. *Seemingly irrelevant decisions* are just what they sound like—they are little decisions that you make every day that may not seem, at the moment, to have any potential impact on your sobriety, because they don't involve drinking or using directly. But they can move you closer to a relapse if you're not aware of them. Let's look at an example:

Jonathan Gets Triggered

Jonathan is a cocaine addict in early recovery. Jonathan was at a friend's house watching the Super Bowl. When his team won, he and his buddies were so excited they wanted to celebrate. His friend Scott suggested that they head down the block to the karaoke bar. Jonathan hesitated for a moment. Since he'd used cocaine and alcohol together in the past, his recovery plan involved abstinence from alcohol as well as cocaine. After a quick deliberation, he thought, *Well, why not? I'll just sip on a soda or something.* When they got there, a bunch of other good friends of theirs were already waiting for them. "Hey, Jonathan!" called an old college buddy, Gregory, from the bar. "I've got your drink all ready for you right here!" When Jonathan walked up, he saw the ice-cold beer sitting there on the table, and it was just too hard to resist. *I'll just have a beer; what's the big deal?* he thought. After one round turned into a few and his friends were still having a good time, one of his buddies told him that he had some cocaine. Although alcohol was not Jonathan's "drug of choice," drinking had been linked with cocaine use for him in the past. That night, Jonathan wound up relapsing on cocaine.

Thinking about Jonathan's relapse, what thoughts come to mind about seemingly irrelevant decisions? For one, Jonathan was not thinking of the bar as a risky place. Going with his buddies to a bar after the game was a decision that was seemingly irrelevant to his recovery from cocaine addiction. This is a common mistake in thinking; when you expose yourself to a substance that is not your "drug of choice," it can still make you vulnerable to relapse to be in a situation where drinking or using are going on, because it takes you outside of the recovery mindset. This is especially true in early recovery, when you are very vulnerable—more so than you might think.

Jonathan also had a plan not to drink alcohol just in case, but that did not work out so well once he was exposed to temptation and social pressure, when his friend had a drink sitting there waiting for him at the bar. This was part of the chain reaction (starting with the decision to go to the bar) that led Jonathan to relapse to cocaine. With alcohol in his system, Jonathan's judgment was not as good as it might have been otherwise. Tracing the situation all the way back to the beginning, Jonathan's seemingly irrelevant decision was going to the bar. If he had opted out of the post-game karaoke bar celebration, he would not have relapsed.

Here are a few suggestions to help you avoid making seemingly irrelevant decisions that will put you at risk:

- Create an awareness of the importance of your moment-to-moment decisions as they affect your recovery.

- Consider your full range of options when confronted with a choice that could impact your ability to stay sober.

- Think about the potential risks and benefits of each choice that you can make.

- Choose the option that will be the most protective of your recovery.

- If you end up choosing a risky option, be prepared with an exit plan or a relapse prevention strategy in place (such as calling a sponsor or supportive friend if you get triggered or bringing someone with you who will help keep you motivated for recovery).

Exercise Promotes Addiction Recovery

As you work your way through this chapter and begin thinking about ways of putting new behaviors into place to increase your chances of recovering successfully, you should be aware of what some of the most recent research on physical exercise in addiction recovery has shown. Everybody knows that physical exercise is good for overall health; you've probably heard somewhere that exercising regularly promotes both physical and mental well-being. The current guidelines from the Centers for Disease Control recommend two hours and thirty minutes of moderate aerobic exercise per week (Centers for Disease Control 2015), which can translate to about thirty minutes of aerobic activity (like walking, jogging, bicycling, or dancing) five days per week. Muscle strengthening exercises (such as resistance training) are also recommended twice per week. Sound tough to commit to? Well, it's true that if you've been out of practice for a while, establishing a consistent regimen is not easy at first. But the exciting news is, there is a good reason to put in the effort: more and more studies have shown that physical exercise has beneficial effects on addiction recovery.

According to a recent series of studies (Rawson et al. 2015; Dolezal et al. 2013; Mooney et al. 2014), people in addiction recovery who do aerobic and muscle strengthening exercise according to the guidelines enjoy many positive mental and physical health benefits: they become more physically fit, they lose weight, they show improvements in psychological symptoms of depression and anxiety, *and* they are more successful in reducing their drug use, compared to a group of addicts in recovery who receive education about health without being involved in a regular exercise program.

In this same series of studies, it was also found that those who exercised during recovery showed changes in their brain cells. They had more of the brain's pleasure chemical, dopamine, available after they exercised regularly for two months. This is important because it means that when you exercise in recovery, it can help restore your ability to experience pleasure and joy—and that can really serve you well, protecting you from one of the most common reasons that people relapse: negative emotions, including feeling unable to enjoy things. Now that new knowledge has shown that physical exercise can help you to stay sober and improve your mental health, it can become a very important and enjoyable part of your recovery plan.

One of the keys to success in making a commitment to exercise is to find something that you actually enjoy doing for exercise. Think about what you enjoy—do you like outdoor activities, like hiking, walking, jogging, or rock climbing? Do you enjoy swimming? Or are you someone who likes to dance, go to the gym and use exercise equipment, or do some other indoor exercise activity? Whatever you try, be sure it isn't something that feels like a chore. If you've had the experience of counting down the minutes until a physical activity is over, then be sure that you don't select that one again! If you can find something you like to do, once you find the time to do it regularly, you won't want to stop. That's the exercise activity you're looking for. Try to work daily exercise into your recovery plan. It will help you feel good about yourself, cope with any negative emotions that might be coming up for you, and stay sober. Now take a moment to think about what kind of activity might work for you to help you get "hooked" on exercise.

Exercise 4.2: Selecting and Committing to an Exercise Activity

Some of the physical activities that I enjoy are:

1. _____

2. _____

3. _____

4. _____

5. _____

I will commit to trying _____ on _____(date).

If it turns out not to be my top choice for a regular exercise activity, as an alternative, I will try

_____ on _____ (date).

Once I select my preferred activity, I will spend _____ minutes on this activity

_____ days per week.

One way to increase the likelihood that you will follow through on your commitment is to keep track of your follow-through on it, and reward yourself for maintaining your commitment. Think of some ways you might reward yourself for exercising. You can do something you enjoy afterward—buy a little something for yourself, enjoy some leisure time with a friend, or do something relaxing (like taking a bubble bath, sunbathing, or watching a favorite TV show). The point is to acknowledge your achievement. And be sure that you make the connection as you reward yourself, telling yourself that the reward is for exercising. You can use the exercise log below to track your progress.

Exercise 4.3: Exercise Log

This log is where you can write down how often you exercise, and record when you reward yourself for it. Try and make a point of rewarding yourself for exercising at least once, if not twice, per week. Use this log as consistently as you can over the next few months, as an aid to establishing a regular exercise regimen.

For the week of: _____

Day	Exercise Type / Minutes Spent	Reward
Monday		
Tuesday		
Wednesday		
Thursday		
Friday		
Saturday		
Sunday		

I met my goals for this week (circle):   Yes   No

I rewarded myself one or more times for exercising (circle):   Yes   No

Taking Stock of Your Social Support Network

Studies show that social support for your recovery has a strong influence on your success in staying clean and sober (Kelly et al. 2012). This means that the more quality relationships you have with people who are supportive of your efforts to stop using alcohol or drugs, the more likely you are to be able to achieve and sustain your sobriety in the long run. Some people come into the recovery process with a lot of loving, supportive people around them who really "get it" and know how to be helpful. But some don't. Some have loving people around, but those people don't really understand their addiction as a disease, and don't know how to support them in the right way. You may have a mix of all of these types of people in your life. Regardless of how your support system may seem right now at this moment, there are ways to build and adjust it, such as:

- Making new friends who are in recovery

- Breaking or limiting contact with friends who are triggering

- Leaning on your existing friends and family who are the most helpful and understanding

- Using assertive communication with the ones who want to help but don't know how (teaching them how to be helpful to you, if they are willing to learn)

- Going to marital or family therapy

The first step is to take stock of the social network that currently exists in your life, and figure out which people, of those you are close to and spend time with, are sources of social support for your recovery, as well as who might be triggering for you. People who are triggering are usually either those who drink or use drugs themselves, and have done so around you, or those who are a source of conflict and negative emotions that ultimately lead to urges to drink or use.

Exercise 4.4: Safety Nets Versus Risky Relationships

In this exercise, you are going to think about whom you might consider a "Safety Net" for you, and which people or relationships are risky. Safety Nets are people who are supportive of your recovery and who won't do things to jeopardize it (such as offering you alcohol or drugs, or behaving in ways that are triggering for you). Risky relationships are those that do the opposite of your Safety Nets—these are relationships with people who would tempt you to use through their own drug or alcohol use, or through their behavior toward you. Take a moment to think about friends, family members, coworkers, a 12-step sponsor, or anyone else who is part of your social network, and list them under the appropriate category.

Safety Nets

1._____

2._____

3._____

4._____

5._____

6._____

Risky Relationships

1._____

2._____

3._____

4._____

5._____

6._____

Now, looking at this list, ask yourself whether you have at least a few solid Safety Nets whom you can count on to support you when you are having a hard day or need someone to talk to. If not, don't despair. There are ways to build this up, which we'll talk about momentarily. Also take a moment now to think about your risky relationships. There are a few ways to deal with the risky people in your life, depending on who they are and how much contact you need to have with them:

- **Avoid:** There are certain risky relationships that you'll want to avoid altogether. Friends with whom your primary connection was all about drinking or using are generally too risky to be around. Dealers or people who used to supply you with drugs are people you should break connections with and avoid.

- **Limit contact:** There may be some risky people you can't avoid entirely (such as coworkers you used to drink or use with after hours), but with whom you can limit your social contact.

- **Set limits:** There may be people (family members, close friends, a spouse, or other loved ones) who are triggering to you but are not people you can or want to avoid altogether. The key in those relationships is to set limits.

Setting Limits: Assertive Communication

Learning to communicate assertively can be a very useful tool in your recovery. First, let's think about what it means to be assertive. There are three different communication styles. On the more reserved extreme, there are *passive* communicators. If you are passive, you tend to:

- Keep your feelings inside

- Avoid making requests of other people

- Keep your wants and needs to yourself

The problem with this communication style is that you can end up letting other people take advantage of you, leading you to feel defeated or resentful because your needs aren't met. And feeling defeated or resentful can fuel other negative emotions, like depression.

If you are at the other extreme, you might be an *aggressive* communicator. If you are aggressive, you tend to:

- Demand what you want

- Take advantage of others

- Deliver your communication with a hostile, rude, or angry tone

The problem with this style is the disrespect it conveys to other people, which also can have the effect of isolating you from others, since it causes others to create distance from you to protect themselves.

Assertive communication is the middle ground that can help you express your needs effectively during your recovery. When you communicate assertively, you:

- Speak respectfully to others

- Can make requests of other people without coming across as demanding

- Praise or thank others for the good or helpful things they do

- Speak your mind in a way that doesn't make others feel put off

- Express yourself in a healthy way, rather than stuffing your feelings

There are many benefits of being assertive. When you are communicating assertively, you are in control of your emotions and your way of expressing them. This inspires respect from others, making it more likely that they will be willing to meet your needs or requests, and inviting healthy and open communication in return. You might be wondering why this is so important for your recovery, and that is a very good question. Let's look at a few scenarios.

Rick's Dilemma

Rick is an alcoholic who has just recently gotten sober. He lives with his girlfriend, Tanya, who is a social drinker. She likes to drink wine with dinner occasionally, and she also likes to host dinner parties, during which she usually serves alcohol. There have been many occasions when, after having friends over, Rick and Tanya have gotten into arguments because of his drinking. Tanya is very happy that Rick is in recovery, but they haven't had any conversations about how she can be helpful to him.

Tanya has continued to drink wine with dinner a few times a week, and she has had a couple of parties recently during which she served alcohol while Rick was around. At the most recent party, Rick was tempted to drink, but he knew that Tanya would get upset if he relapsed. So he waited until she fell asleep that night, and with the urge still very strong, he went into the kitchen and poured himself a drink for the first time in over a month. He ended up having five drinks that night before he went to bed.

Rick's situation is a common one. It is very difficult to go into recovery and succeed in your efforts to avoid drinking or using when a partner or close friend continues to actively drink or use around you. At the beginning of this chapter, we discussed the importance of removing alcohol, drugs, or anything in your environment that is associated with drinking or using, to eliminate as many temptations or relapse triggers as possible. By keeping quiet about the way that exposure to alcohol at home is affecting him, Rick is being *passive* by not expressing his need for adjustments to Tanya. There could be a couple of reasons for this:

- Rick may not like the idea of "burdening" his girlfriend or anyone else with his recovery.

- Rick may worry that Tanya won't want to be with him if it means limiting her use of alcohol or making adjustments to her lifestyle.

- Rick feels that he should be "strong enough" to have alcohol around him without relapsing.

Do any of these ideas sound familiar? These types of thoughts are often the reasons why people in recovery don't express their needs openly. At the root of the thoughts is the belief that they will be rejected in some way if they ask too much of others, or the belief that they should be "stronger" than the addiction (and therefore should not have any needs from other people related to their addiction recovery). These are what we call *recovery-interfering thoughts*, ones that stand in the way of your success in recovery. So, how do you overcome these ways of thinking? Well, first, you have to recognize them when they occur. Then, you can try having a healthier inner dialogue to cope with these thoughts and try to change them. Coming back to Rick's situation, here are some healthy ways he can talk himself through the recovery-interfering thoughts that prevent him from asking Tanya for her help (by making some adjustments, such as removing alcohol from the house):

- **Recovery-interfering thought:** *I don't want to burden my girlfriend with my recovery.*

  Assertive, recovery mindset: Although it might be burdensome to her to make some changes, the effect that Rick's addiction has had on his relationship has been way more burdensome, and could create more serious problems. If she cares about him, she will make whatever adjustments are needed to help him. And she won't necessarily feel burdened; maybe she has been waiting for Rick to come up with one or more ways that she can help him. You never know how another person feels until you sit down and have a conversation about it.

- **Recovery-interfering thought:** *She might not want to be with me if she has to make adjustments to her lifestyle.*

   Assertive, recovery mindset: Hopefully Tanya will not feel turned off by the idea of making some changes to her lifestyle in support of Rick's recovery—such as not keeping alcohol in the house for the time being, and hosting alcohol-free dinners, or hosting dinners at a restaurant. But if she does object, then she may need to become more knowledgeable about addiction. If she doesn't know much about it, she may find it difficult to understand why Rick can't just control himself when there is alcohol at home. To educate herself, she can go with him to counseling, or attend an Al-Anon meeting. Regardless, for their relationship to be successful, Tanya will need to deepen her understanding of Rick's addiction, and figure out whether and how she might be willing to support his recovery.

- **Recovery-interfering thought:** *I should be strong enough to be around alcohol without relapsing.*

   Assertive, recovery mindset: Remember, "Be smart, not strong!" Even if Rick thinks that he *should* be strong enough to exercise willpower and resist drinking when there is alcohol in his home, the reality is, he isn't. He has an addiction and he's in early recovery. The way to preserve his recovery is to be smart and remove all triggers from his environment, rather than trying to prove that he can handle being around alcohol. Accepting that reality is a big part of recovery.

Now that you know how to talk yourself through some of the thoughts that can interfere with being assertive, you'll need some practice in the delivery of assertive communication. Here are some rules of thumb:

Listen Carefully

When you show others that you are listening to them, it helps strengthen the connection between you, so that both you and the person you are talking to can be open about your feelings, including your wants and needs. There are both verbal and non-verbal ways of showing someone that you are listening. Here are some examples of verbal listening skills:

- Asking questions to clarify your understanding of what the other person is saying (such as asking "Why?" or "How?" or "Can you say a little more about what you mean by that?")

- Summarizing (or paraphrasing) your understanding of what the person has said to you (for example, "If I heard you right, then you feel like...")

- Using "I" statements when you eventually respond, so that you come across as owning your feelings and avoid blaming or making false assumptions about the other person. (For example, rather than saying something like, "Your anger triggers me to want to use," you could say, "Sometimes I feel like you're angry with me. And I don't cope with that very well. When I feel you're angry with me, I get the urge to use." Notice how much "I" is used in the assertive statement; that is much less likely to put the other person on the defense.)

Nonverbal skills are also important tools to show another person that you are listening. A few ways that you can show someone you are listening through your body language are:

- Making eye contact

- Using facial movement and expressions to show your interest—such as nodding and smiling when the other person is talking

- Leaning toward the other person, or positioning yourself in a way that shows you're tuning in

- Keeping distractions (such as your cell phone) out of reach during your conversation

Ask for What You Need

Once you've shown the other person you're talking to that you are tuned in and listening, if there is something that you feel that you need, you can request it in a respectful way. One way to do this is to express your feelings as they relate to what you're asking for. The phrase would look like this:

I feel _____ when _____ , and

I need _____ .

Putting it all together, let's come back to Rick's situation. Using the way of phrasing his request suggested above, his assertive conversation with Tanya might go something like this: "I've been doing a lot of work on my recovery, and I'm learning about some of the things that I need to be successful. You've been very supportive of my recovery, and because I trust you and I know your intentions for me are good, I need to tell you something that isn't so easy for me to admit. *I feel* <u>very vulnerable</u> *when* <u>I am around alcohol. I've noticed that having it around the house and having people drinking at dinner parties here is hard for me. I get strong cravings to drink. I am worried that I am going to relapse,</u> *and I need* <u>your help and support. Would you be willing to consider not keeping alcohol at home for the time being?</u>"

In this example, Rick used a lot of the key skills involved in assertive communication:

- He started the discussion by saying something positive to Tanya about what he appreciates about her ("You've been very supportive…").

- He made several "I" statements, underlined above, about his feelings of vulnerability to relapse around alcohol (without accusing Tanya and her use of alcohol of being the reason that he is triggered).

- He expressed his own concerns also underlined, about the effect that having alcohol in the house could have on his recovery.

- He made a direct request for Tanya's help and support ("and I need your help and support. Would you be willing…").

Most importantly, he did all of this in a very polite and respectful manner.

In your own recovery, there may be ways you need to set limits with others that are completely different from Rick's situation. Some of the ways that you might use the assertiveness skills you are learning include:

- Asking people close to you who have been affected by your addiction *not* to *repeatedly* bring up the ways that they've been hurt or upset by your addictive behaviors

- Asking your loved ones to be patient with you during your recovery if you are emotionally up and down or if you need some time to yourself

- Explaining how certain behaviors of others (such as arguing, criticizing, or bringing up the past) may be triggering for you and asking that your partner, family, or loved ones try to minimize them

- Asking a loved one to come to counseling with you to better understand how to support your recovery

Exercise 4.5: Practice Assertive Communication

To get some practice with assertive communication, in this exercise you will think about a few people in your life with whom you might need to set some limits or make some requests related to your recovery. For each of these people, you will practice writing out how you would express your needs using assertive communication.

Person 1: _____

What I need from this person: _____

Here's how I'll say it assertively:

I feel _____ when _____

_____.

I need _____

_____.

Person 2: _____

What I need from this person: _____

Here's how I'll say it assertively:

I feel _____ when _____

_____.

I need _____

_____.

Saying No to Offers of Alcohol or Drugs

Social pressure to drink or use causes one in three people in recovery to slip (Epstein and McCrady 2009). There are various reasons why it might be challenging for you to turn down these offers: It might be because the urge to use once it's available is so strong, it is hard for you to overcome it. Another reason is that you may not be good at saying no to someone who is pushy. (And some people are alcohol or drug "pushers.") You might also worry about what judgments other people might make about you if you say no.

The most important thing to remember in all of these situations is that your recovery is your priority, and the temptation to drink or use to please others is something you'll need to overcome promptly if you're going to stay sober. Drink or drug "pushers" need to be addressed respectfully but firmly so that they don't continue to offer and trigger you. Here's how to say no, whether to a pusher or to a friendly offer of alcohol or drugs:

- The first thing to say in response to an offer is "no" or "no thank you" in a serious tone, so that you come across as direct and clear and not "wishy washy" about your decision.

- Make eye contact when you say no; otherwise you might appear uncertain of your answer, leaving the door open for the other person to convince you to change your mind.

- Ask for something else instead: "No, thank you. Do you have sparkling water? That would be great." Or if someone is offering an activity involving drug use, you can suggest something else that is not so risky. For example, if a friend suggests that you go to his house and smoke some weed, you could say, "No, thanks. I'm hungry, though. Do you want to go out and get something to eat?"

- Try changing the subject.

- Ask the person not to offer you alcohol or drugs anymore. Say, "I stopped drinking," or "I've stopped using," and assertively ask the person not to offer any to you. Remember that anyone who continues to offer is not being respectful to you, and you might not want to spend a lot of time around that person.

- Have a dialogue with yourself about it. Remind yourself why your recovery is so important. You shouldn't feel guilty about letting others down by not joining them in drinking or using. That's a choice they are making for themselves. But you are choosing to build a healthy life for yourself, and you deserve that. Part of recovery is learning to be self-protective.

If you have a friend, sponsor, counselor, or loved one who would be willing, try pairing up and practicing what you will say when you are offered alcohol or drugs. It's only a matter of time before that happens, and the more prepared you are, the better you will handle it.

Expanding Your Social Network

In this section, we will focus on ways of building up your network of support so that you have at least a handful of Safety Nets you can count on to help you through a tough moment, day, or period during your recovery.

First, remember that there are a lot of different types of relationships that can be Safety Nets for you. Your family members—including children, parents, and other relatives—can be Safety Nets. Members of a self-help group or other community-based organization (such as a church or temple), professional counselors, friends, or a romantic partner are other possible Safety Nets. The first thing to pay attention to as you identify who, for you, is a Safety Net, is the role of alcohol and drugs in that person's life. Is this someone who drinks or uses drugs heavily, or who is likely to drink or use when around you? Is it someone who would be willing to abstain from drinking or using when around you? Ideally, your Safety Nets should be people who either don't drink or use (or do so very little), or who are willing to abstain around you.

The next step is for you to think about the qualities that you are looking for in the people who could be Safety Nets in your life. Use the exercise below to help you identify these qualities.

Exercise 4.6: Qualities of Safety Nets

People who can be Safety Nets for me will have the following qualities (check all that apply for you):

_____ Not actively drinking or using

_____ Good at listening

_____ Knowledgeable about addiction (or willing to learn)

_____ Respectful toward me

_____ Nonjudgmental

_____ Trustworthy

_____ Kind

_____ Nurturing

_____ Patient

_____ Willing to make time for me

_____ Not flaky

_____ Genuine

_____ Interested in sharing thoughts, perspectives, and ideas

_____ Protective of me and my recovery

Other important qualities of a Safety Net in my life:

_____

_____

_____

_____

If you don't currently have any Safety Nets in your life, or if you have just a few and would like to have more, make it a priority to expand your support network. Having many people to call on for support when you need it is invaluable in any stage of recovery.

Exercise 4.7: Ways to Expand Your Network

In this exercise, you will list new ways that you plan to try to expand your social support network.

List at least two ways you can reach out to old friends or potential new ones, such as joining a volunteer organization, enrolling in a class, or contacting one or more old friends who are potential Safety Nets:

_____

_____

_____

_____

_____

List at least two ways you can become part of a community-based organization, such as joining a mutual self-help group like Alcoholics Anonymous (AA) or Narcotics Anonymous (NA); attending a religious activity at a temple, church, or other entity; joining a special-interest group or club; or seeking a professional counselor or other treatment provider:

_____

_____

_____

_____

List at least one way that you can deepen your relationship with one or more of your family members (a partner, children, or other relatives), such as calling or getting together more often:

_____

_____

_____

_____

A Word on Mutual Self-Help Programs

Mutual self-help groups are the most widely available and helpful resources that you can use to build a social support network for your recovery. More and more studies show that participating in self-help groups enhances social support for recovery, and as a result, contributes in a very meaningful way to success in achieving and maintaining sobriety (Kelly et al. 2012). There are various self-help groups that use the 12-step recovery model, including Alcoholics Anonymous, Narcotics Anonymous, Marijuana Anonymous, and Dual Recovery Anonymous (for people with both addictions and mental health problems), to name just a few. Other self-help groups include Self-Management and Recovery Training (SMART Recovery), an alternative that may be a good fit for people who are uncomfortable with the spiritual component of 12-step groups.

It might help to keep the following information and advice in mind as you explore self-help groups:

- Some people like AA and other 12-step groups and others don't. It is not for everybody, but for those who get something out of it, there is potential for great benefits.

- You don't have to agree with everything you hear in a 12-step group for it to be helpful. Remember, it is the social support that is at the core of the therapeutic benefit, so even if the twelve steps themselves are not all helpful to you, getting connected with other people in recovery is likely to be therapeutic in itself.

- Try going to lots of different meetings. Most people need to attend several different meetings before they find the one that feels like a good fit. There are different formats to explore. (For example, there are speaker meetings, in which individuals talk about their experience to the group of attendees, and there are step study meetings, in which one of the twelve steps is discussed in depth, and the group will be involved in discussion.)

- Get involved beyond just attending, if you can. Plan to get a sponsor, or volunteer to take a "commitment" at a meeting (like setting up chairs or coffee). Studies show that people who get more involved in these ways get more long-term benefits and have more success in staying sober (Timko 2006).

• If you don't like the spiritual part of the 12-step meetings, try going to a SMART Recovery meeting, which is more CBT-based.

Wrap-up

Congratulations on working your way through an intense chapter with lots of new concepts and skills to work on! As you're learning, there are a lot of different ways that you can lay the groundwork for a recovery-oriented life. It starts with making your environment safe and free from triggers. Then, you have to start thinking with your recovery mindset about your day-to-day decisions, to be sure that you are not setting yourself up for a relapse without realizing it. Next thing you know, you're rethinking your relationships to figure out who's good for your recovery and who is not so good, and you're adjusting your communication style with the not-so-good ones. Then you're looking to make new friends, join new organizations, and go to self-help meetings. And don't forget to exercise!

If all of this is a little overwhelming, that is completely understandable. But remember, you don't have to make all of these changes at once. Pace yourself with each of these skills and the exercises that go along with them in a way that's comfortable for you. Once you've put them into practice, you can move on to the next chapter, where you'll learn to be a "self expert," so that you can begin to understand how your personal ways of thinking can set you up for a relapse, and learn how to change them.

CHAPTER 5

Step 3: Become a "Self Expert"

Now that you have done the hard work of taking an honest look at the problems that your drug or alcohol use has caused, strengthening your motivation to change, and creating your change plan, it is important for you to learn to truly know your addicted self. *What does that mean?* you might ask. Think back to when we talked about your "addicted brain" and how it drives you to act in destructive ways that support your addiction. Step 3 is the first major step you will take to strengthen your "rational brain" and put it into the driver's seat.

To do this, you need to know your addicted self inside and out. That means knowing exactly how, when, and why your addicted brain is most likely to get triggered and start competing with your rational, recovering brain for control. Once you have that figured out, you will be a "self expert." In this chapter, you will begin to learn how to use cognitive and behavioral therapy skills to understand your own unique patterns of thinking and feeling as they relate to your addiction.

The purpose of this chapter is to teach you three strategies that can help you to identify the situations and ways of thinking that fuel your addictive behavior: (1) identifying your unique triggers for alcohol or drug use, (2) recognizing distorted thinking, and (3) using self-monitoring skills. The more frequently you are able to recognize and anticipate when your addicted brain is taking hold and causing you to think and act in irrational, self-destructive ways, the better you will get at intentionally using your rational brain to make healthier choices for yourself. Each time your rational brain wins control over your behavior, your recovery gets a little bit stronger and your addicted brain loses a little bit of power over your behavior. In the long term, your rational brain can take over completely, so that making healthy choices is no longer a fight; it is a way of life. In this chapter, and the next, you will learn how to use cognitive and behavioral therapy skills to become a "self expert" and reclaim that control.

Becoming a "self expert" is a process of understanding how your addiction controls you, so that, with time and practice, you can turn the tables on it. That means getting a handle on the wide range of situations, places, people, and experiences that activate your addicted brain. These are called *triggers*. Typically, when you encounter a trigger, this causes a sequence of experiences that leads to drug or alcohol use when your addicted brain is in control. Here's how it unfolds:

TRIGGER → THOUGHT → CRAVING → DRUG OR ALCOHOL USE

Does this sequence look familiar? If it does, that's great! If it doesn't, that is perfectly okay; for many people with addictions, this process happens so quickly that it takes time and practice just to notice it. This practice is a very important part of the cognitive behavioral approach. As you progress through the exercises in this chapter, you will learn to notice when you are triggered, and what exactly that feels like for you. For instance, when you are triggered, you may or may not be aware of the thoughts that are going through your head. You may or may not have noticed exactly what the trigger was. Maybe you are simply aware of an urge or craving to drink or use drugs, and if so, that is a great start.

As you will learn, there are many components of cravings and people experience them differently. Some people feel cravings physically in their bodies, while for others the craving is more of a thought process, like *I need it* or *I can't handle these feelings without it*. When you learn to self-monitor, you will be able to look at the diagram above and know exactly what happened during the sequence of *TRIGGER* → *THOUGHT* → *CRAVING*—physically, emotionally, and *cognitively* (which refers to the thoughts you were having). Once you are aware of what happened, you can begin an inner dialogue with yourself about it, and you can use this inner dialogue to cope with the thoughts, feelings, and cravings without drinking or using drugs.

Another key component of becoming a "self expert" is developing an awareness of the kinds of things your addicted brain will tell you to get you to drink or use drugs. In CBT, these distorted or irrational thoughts are called *red flag thoughts*. In this chapter, you will learn about some red flag thoughts that a lot of people with addictions experience when they are feeling triggered. In reviewing these thoughts, you can identify the ones that you've had, or even come up with your own. This will prepare you for the next chapter, where you will learn how to "talk back" to the thoughts using your rational, recovering brain.

Triggers and Urges

At one time or another, most everyone in recovery experiences urges to drink or use drugs. In fact, cravings are one of the symptoms that define the disease of addiction (American Psychiatric Association 2013). That's no surprise, of course; there are both biological and psychological explanations for why you would feel a desire to drink or use drugs after your last drink or dose has left your body. Physically, when you are addicted to something, your body becomes dependent on having a steady, consistent dose of it in your system. When that steady dose is diminished, or taken away abruptly, your addicted brain will communicate urges to you to get you to replenish it. This is because, as your body is adjusting to receiving less of the substance, you can experience uncomfortable physical and mental withdrawal symptoms. The conditioned, addicted part of your brain will tell you that you need to drink or use to get back to feeling normal. That's the cycle of withdrawal.

The psychological urge or craving can feel just as potent—and sometimes even stronger. You may recall that in chapter 2, you learned about how your use of alcohol or drugs can become a conditioned, automatic response to certain cues, much like a habit. When drinking or using drugs becomes associated, or "linked," with certain situations, emotions, people, or things, then those become triggers. Because that psychological link between triggers and using substances can be very powerful, being in the presence of these triggers can become quite uncomfortable without alcohol or drugs. You'll experience this discomfort as a craving.

Studies have shown that triggers fall into several categories (Marlatt and Gordon 1985; Larimer, Palmer, and Marlatt 1999). As you become a self expert, think about which of these categories apply to you, so that you can learn to become more self-aware when you enter triggering situations:

- **Negative emotional states:** Some people drink or use drugs as a way of "self-medicating" uncomfortable emotions such as anxiety, sadness, boredom, loneliness, or anger.

- **Interpersonal conflict:** Have you ever used alcohol or drugs to cope with a relationship problem? This is another category of triggers—some people drink or use when they have a fight with a partner or a family member. Others get triggered by rejection or criticism at work, school, or home. Often it is the combination of a conflict and your emotional *reaction* to it that places you at risk for a relapse. In other words, it's not just the fight with your partner; it's also the emotion (for example, anger) that it generates that then leads you to drink or use drugs to cope. In fact, in one of the largest studies of the reasons people with addictions relapse (Marlatt 1996), more than 50 percent of the relapses were triggered by negative emotional states stemming from interpersonal conflict. If interpersonal problems are a trigger for you, then finding a healthier place to put the anger or other negative emotions that arise is going to be an important part of your recovery.

- **Social pressure:** Do you feel like you just can't resist drinking or using when you are in a social situation where other people are indulging? If so, you are not alone. For some people, these are the most challenging situations when trying to abstain from alcohol or drug use. To overcome this challenge, you first need to understand *why* this situation is difficult for you. For some people, it is hard to refuse an offer of alcohol or drugs simply because it is so tempting. For others, self-consciousness can take over, leading them to feel worried about how others will think about them or judge them if they make different choices. This is a very natural tendency but it is an important one to work through in your recovery. Social pressures to use substances can be direct (for example, someone offering you a drink or drugs), or indirect (as in being around people who you know have drugs or who are drinking or using in front of you). You will learn how to respond to these kinds of social pressures in the next chapter.

- **Positive emotions:** For some people, drinking and drug use is all about amplifying the good feelings, rather than escaping from or avoiding an uncomfortable feeling. Maybe you get triggered when you're at a celebration, or when you are in a very good mood. Or maybe when something reminds you of the positive emotions or sensations that drinking or using can bring on for you, you experience a desire to feel those things (like relaxation, elation, confidence, or an energy boost). If this is you, then one of your goals will be to find other sources of positive emotions and rewarding experiences or activities that are compatible with your recovery. Another important goal will be to learn to think more carefully about the full range of effects that you can expect drinking or using drugs to have on you. If you think it all the way through, you'll find that the positive sensations are only part of the story. You will practice thinking it all the way through in the next chapter.

Exercise 5.1: Identifying Triggers

Below you will find a list of triggers that can initiate the sequence of thoughts, cravings, and behaviors (like drinking or using drugs) that we have been reviewing. Place a check mark beside the triggers that you have experienced, and place a star next to the ones that you feel come up repeatedly for you. You'll notice that we've separated internal from external triggers, so that you can start to learn to distinguish between them. Remember that internal triggers are just what they sound like; they are emotions inside of you. External triggers, on the other hand, are cues that are external to you—such as places, people, or situations that you have come to associate with drinking or using.

Internal Triggers

_____   Depression

_____   Loneliness

_____   Happiness

_____   Excitement

_____   Feeling stressed

_____   Feeling irritable

_____   Feeling overwhelmed

_____   Feeling jealous

_____   Anxiety

_____   Boredom

_____   Anger

_____   Feeling rejected

_____   Frustration

_____   Guilt or shame

_____   Needing an energy boost

_____   Withdrawal symptoms

Other internal triggers: _____

_____

_____

_____

_____

External Triggers

In this exercise, we focus on four types of external triggers: people, places, situations or activities, and things. Under each category, place a check mark beside the triggers that apply to you, and place a star next to those that come up repeatedly for you.

People

_____   Friends

_____   Spouse or significant other

_____   Family members

_____   Coworkers or bosses

List of people who trigger me: _____

_____

_____

_____

_____

Places

_____ Bars or clubs

_____ Friends' houses (name those friends here):

_____

_____

_____

_____

_____ Concerts

_____ School or work

_____ Neighborhoods or freeway exits

Other places that are triggers for me: _____

_____

_____

_____

_____

Situations or Activities

_____ Parties (or other gatherings at which you meet new people)

_____ Holidays or other special occasions

_____ When home alone

_____ When dining out

_____ Before or during a date

_____ Waking up in the morning

_____ After work or school

Other situations or activities that are triggers for me: _____

_____

_____

_____

_____

Things

_____ Stashes of alcohol or drugs in the house

_____ Paraphernalia associated with drinking or using (favorite shot glasses or wine glasses, bongs, rolling paper, pipes, or other objects used as part of rituals when getting high)

Other things that are triggers for me: _____

_____

_____

_____

_____

The Role of Thoughts in Relapse

Now that you have learned what your triggers are, you are ready for the next step: uncovering the thoughts that lead you to drink or use. Remember, the usual sequence that can end in a relapse is: TRIGGER → THOUGHT → CRAVING → DRUG OR ALCOHOL USE. In the exercises that follow, you will start connecting your personal triggers with specific thoughts.

In everyday life, our thoughts are directly connected to our emotions and our actions. We all have some thoughts that are rational and some that are irrational. As someone with an addiction, your irrational thoughts around drinking or using mostly come from your addicted brain. Thoughts are very important to notice and understand, because when we encounter a trigger—or any stressful or unexpected situation—the way we think about it dictates the way that we cope with it (Marlatt and Gordon 1985). Let's look at an example.

Scott Gets Triggered

Scott is a software engineer with alcoholism. He has been abstinent from alcohol for two months and is doing well in his recovery. One day, he goes to work and his boss asks to meet with him. Scott's boss says that one of the clients he has been working with is complaining that he has been too slow to resolve problems with his new software, and that he was not very polite in his email when this issue was raised. Scott's boss is writing him up, and warns him that he needs to improve his efficiency and customer service to meet performance standards.

So, there it is: a triggering interpersonal situation. Scott feels devalued by his boss, leading him to feel inadequate both personally and professionally. Ideally, Scott would respond to this with some positive coping skills, like finding a healthy outlet for the emotions that this feedback from his boss brought on. He might try to resolve things with the client who is upset, and find a way to communicate with his boss constructively to improve his standing at work. But Scott's ability to take these actions depends on the way that he is thinking about the situation, and himself. Let's take a look at some of the thoughts that go through Scott's head after his talk with his boss.

- *He is picking on me. This just isn't fair!*

- *I didn't do anything wrong with that client. I wish I didn't have to deal with him.*

- *Nothing I do is ever good enough.*

- *I never succeed at anything. I knew it was just a matter of time before I'd get fired from this place.*

- *My boss probably just doesn't like me. Nobody likes me.*

- *If I could just have one drink, it would calm me down.*

Scott is stuck in a cycle of negative and irrational thinking. You might notice as you look at each of his thoughts that he is not stepping back from the situation to try and evaluate whether there is anything constructive about the feedback his boss gave him, or whether there is a way to get some resolution to the problem. Instead, his irrational thoughts take hold; he is quick to interpret many aspects of the situation as reflections of his own personal inadequacy. It's as though he is overly sensitive to any aspects of the situation that could reflect rejection and negativity. Looking at life from this irrational perspective, it is not surprising that he feels like a failure—an unlikable and unsuccessful person—and that he predicts that he will be fired.

Scott is not alone; a lot of people (both addicts and non-addicts) can get easily swept into this irrational way of interpreting and reacting to an upsetting experience. The key is to recognize what is happening and prevent yourself from "falling for it." It is, after all, irrational! If you fall for it, your actions will be irrational too. If you catch those thoughts when they happen, you can switch gears, engage your rational brain, and use some positive coping strategies that will lead you *away* from a relapse. Let's break it down further so that you can figure out your own patterns of distorted thinking.

Distorted Thoughts—Learn to Catch Them!

There are certain types of distorted or irrational thoughts that make you more vulnerable to relapse. Like Scott's distorted thoughts, some are directly related to drinking or using, while others are not. It's important for you to know that even the thoughts that are not directly related to drinking or using can lead you to a relapse. In Scott's situation, some of the negative, irrational thoughts he has about himself (such as *Nobody likes me*) trigger negative emotions, which he experiences as feelings of worthlessness. These negative emotions lead him to have thoughts about drinking.

Have you ever had thoughts about drinking or using after something upsetting happened to you? If so, it was not just the upsetting event or situation that created the desire to drink or use; it was the thoughts and emotions that you experienced during or after the event. Picture the most recent upsetting event that got you thinking about drinking or using. Can you pinpoint the thoughts you had in that situation, just before you started thinking about drinking or using? If so, that is terrific! If not, don't worry, you'll get plenty of practice with this.

For some, the hardest part of overcoming irrational thinking is recognizing when it is happening. That is because most of our irrational thought patterns have repeated themselves so often over time that they have become automatic. When our thoughts are automatic, we tend not to notice them. As a "self expert in training," you are going to learn to "catch" your thoughts as they happen. Let's take a look at some of the most common types of irrational thoughts so that you can start to identify the ones that you'll need to work on.

Red Flag Thoughts

Because they are directly related to drinking or using, red flag thoughts may be easier for you to "catch" than other thoughts that can lead you to relapse. A red flag thought is something that you tell yourself about drinking or using that increases the likelihood that you will relapse. In CBT, sometimes these are referred to as "relapse justifying" thoughts or a process of "relapse justification." In the example above, Scott's red flag thought is, *If I could just have one drink, it would calm me down.* These types of thoughts, that "make it okay" for you to drink or use when you are in recovery, are coming from your addicted brain. When you find yourself having these thoughts that give you "permission" to drink or use, that's when you have to work harder to kick your rational brain into gear and use your new coping skills, which you will learn in steps 4 through 7. Your job right now is just to notice the thoughts as they happen.

Exercise 5.2: Identifying Red Flag Thoughts

The following is a list of some common red flag thoughts (Brown et al. 2006). Check all that you've had at one time or another and add any that you don't see listed.

_____ *I have to… (I have to have a drink.)*

_____ *Nobody has to know.*

_____ *It really doesn't matter if… (It really doesn't matter if I use.)*

_____ *I can control it.*

_____ *I'm only going to have one.*

_____ *I'm having a bad day; I might as well use.*

_____ *I deserve to… (I deserve to have a drink.)*

_____ *It's a special occasion! I can always start over tomorrow.*

Other red flag thoughts I've had: _____

_____

_____

_____

Mistakes in Thinking

Now that you have a better handle on your red flag thoughts, it's time to take a look at other common mistakes in thinking. Take a look at the six common types of irrational thoughts that follow, noticing the ones that you relate to the most. Keep in mind that not everyone experiences every type of irrational thought; if you notice that there are some types of irrational thoughts you are unfamiliar with, then you don't need to come up with a personal example for those.

BLACK-OR-WHITE THINKING

When you see things in black and white, it means that they are either completely good or completely bad. Scott was caught up in a lot of black-or-white thinking just before he started entertaining the idea of drinking. When his boss gave him critical feedback, he started to view himself as completely worthless on the job and a failure—with thoughts such as *Nothing I do is ever good enough,* and *I never succeed at anything.* When your thoughts contain words like *nothing* and *never,* then you're definitely in the thick of some black-or-white thinking. If you're a perfectionist type, you're more vulnerable to this; like Scott, making a mistake causes you to view everything you've done as useless. Let's look at an example of how black-or-white thinking can lead to a red flag thought.

Black-or-White Thought	Red Flag Thought
I messed up everything at work.	*I might as well go and drink.*

Now, try writing down one or more examples of your black-or-white thoughts and the red flag thoughts they can lead to.

Examples of black-or-while thoughts I've had: _____

_____

_____

Red flag thought: _____

_____

_____

DISCOUNTING THE POSITIVE

Picture yourself wearing a pair of glasses with a screen in place of the lens. You filter your interpretations of experiences, situations, and the ways that people interact with you through this screen. The screen keeps all of the positive thoughts about your experiences on the outside, letting only the negative thoughts come through. This is the case even when good things happen. For example, if Scott's boss gives him a compliment on something he did well at work, and he's "discounting the positive," he might have a thought like, *He didn't mean that. He just feels sorry for me because I keep on screwing up. He said that out of pity.* By discounting the positive, Scott is casting aside all of the ways that this compliment might be reassuring. Below is an example of how discounting the positive can lead to a red flag thought.

Discounting the Positive	Red Flag Thought
My boss only said something nice to me out of pity.	*I'm pathetic. I have nothing to lose by drinking.*

Now, try writing down one or more examples of thoughts you've had that discount the positive. Then, write down the red flag thoughts they can lead to.

Thoughts that discount the positive: _____

_____

_____

Red flag thoughts: _____

_____

_____

JUMPING TO CONCLUSIONS

If you tend to jump to conclusions, you are doing one of two things: You are either *mind reading* or *fortune telling*. If you are a mind reader, then you assume that other people's behavior toward you reflects something negative about how they feel about you. You make these interpretations with very little or no factual information. For example, if you are with a friend who is not being especially talkative, rather than assuming that your friend might be having a bad day, or might have something on her mind, you think, *She's not talking to me because she doesn't like me.* That is one form of jumping to conclusions.

If you fall into a habit of *fortune telling,* then you predict that things will turn out badly for you. The way you see things, there is doom and gloom waiting for you around the corner; that is your ultimate fate. Scott did some fortune telling after his boss gave him the negative feedback; he predicted that he would get fired, even though his boss did not say that he was on the road to losing his job. Although getting written up at work obviously isn't a positive, it is also not a sure path to getting fired. When you are fortune telling, you go straight to the worst-case scenario without considering the other possible outcomes.

Let's look at a couple of examples of how jumping to conclusions can bring on red flag thoughts. You'll notice that in the first example below, the red flag thought is one that is triggered by interpersonal conflict; sometimes you may feel like retaliating against someone who has upset you, by drinking or using. Make a mental note of it or write down an example in the exercise below if this is a pattern of thinking you have experienced before. In steps 4 through 7, you will learn how to cope with interpersonal conflict in a healthier way.

Jumping to Conclusions	Red Flag Thought
My brother is blowing me off because he thinks he's better than me. (Mind reading)	*I'll show him! If he's going to treat me like that, I'm going to go use.*
With my luck, treatment won't work for me. (Fortune telling)	*I'll never be able to stay clean and sober. There's no point in even trying.*

Now, try writing down one or more examples of ways that you have engaged in jumping to conclusions, and the red flag thoughts that are connected.

My ways of jumping to conclusions (mind reading or fortune telling): _____

_____

_____

Red flag thoughts: _____

_____

_____

TAKING YOUR FEELINGS TOO SERIOUSLY

When you take your feelings too seriously, it means that you think of your feelings as reality. Even though your feelings are real, they can lead you to some unrealistic conclusions if you take them too seriously. For example, if you feel depressed you may draw the conclusion that you can't enjoy anything. Although your depressed feeling is real, if you were to get out and try to do something enjoyable, chances are it would help you get out of that mood.

Here's another example: Scott felt worthless at work after his boss spoke with him about his need for improvement. Just because he *felt* worthless, it doesn't mean that he *is* worthless. It is hard to separate an intense feeling from reality during the moment, but the fact is that just because you feel a certain way, it doesn't mean that you *are* that way. Let's look at an example of how taking your feelings too seriously can lead to a red flag thought.

Taking Your Feelings Too Seriously	Red Flag Thought
I feel hopeless; therefore, life must be hopeless for me.	*Things will never get better. At least if I go use I won't have to feel the pain of my hopeless life.*

Now, try writing down one or more examples of your experience with taking your feelings too seriously, and the red flag thoughts that this can lead to.

Examples of my thoughts when I've taken my feelings too seriously: _____

_____

_____

Red flag thoughts: _____   _____

_____

_____

SELF-BLAME

If you tend to be hard on yourself, and have an active self-critical voice inside of you, then you probably can relate to this mistake in thinking. You blame yourself for things that may not be in your control. Your addiction is a perfect example. Do you ever blame yourself for it? Remember, even if you have made bad choices during your fight with addiction, becoming an addict was not your choice; nor was it your fault. You developed a brain disease, and you are working very hard to overcome it and put your rational mind back in control. Let's look at an example of how self-blame can lead to a red flag thought.

Self-Blaming Thought	Red Flag Thought
It's all my fault that I drink too much.	*I've ruined my life; I have nothing to lose by continuing to drink.*

Now, try writing down one or more examples of your self-blaming thinking and the red flag thoughts that it can lead to.

Self-blaming thoughts: _____

_____

_____

Red flag thoughts: _____

_____

_____

LABELING YOURSELF

Labeling yourself is a close relative to taking your feelings too seriously. *I feel _____; therefore I must be _____.* You label yourself for the ways that you feel, or for the mistakes that you've made. For example, if you are feeling down, you might think, *I'm a depressing person; I'm such a downer for everybody.* Instead of thinking of yourself as a person who happens to be in a depressed mood, you label yourself for it. Another example: if you make a mistake, you might label yourself as a "loser," rather than a person who happened to make a mistake. Let's look at an example of how labeling can lead to a red flag thought.

Labeling Thought	Red Flag Thought
I relapsed, just like I knew I would. I'm just a raging addict, always will be.	*Raging addicts like me never get clean in the long run. I'm going to be another bad statistic. There's no point in me even trying to stay clean.*

Now, try writing down one or more examples of your own experience with labeling and the red flag thoughts that it can lead to.

Labeling thoughts: _____

_____

_____

Red flag thoughts: _____

_____

_____

_____

The Spiraling Lapse

If you're like most people who struggle with addictions, then you've probably made more than one attempt to cut back or stop drinking or using. Think about the last time that you tried, unsuccessfully, to stop drinking or using. Did you know that the first time you drank or used after days, weeks, or months of abstinence was *not* a relapse? That very first time that you drink or use after a period of going without is called a *slip* or a *lapse*. What you probably don't know is that, when you *lapse,* the way that you talk to yourself about it can determine whether or not you will continue drinking or using. When you keep the lapse going, it turns into a *relapse.*

Research has shown that it is very common to think about lapses in ways that keep you on the path to relapse, rather than recovery (Marlatt and Gordon 1985). Although it's true that a lapse places you at risk for a relapse, the relapse is *not* inevitable. You have more control than you might think over the outcome. To prevent a lapse from converting into a full-blown relapse, you need to avoid the mistake called the *spiraling lapse*. The *spiraling lapse* is when you interpret a lapse as being the result of one of two things:

1. You see yourself as a personal failure. People who interpret a lapse as a personal failure tend to feel very guilty or ashamed, and the desire to avoid or numb those feelings can very easily lead to more drinking or using.

2: You view the lapse as being the result of things that are completely beyond your control. People who think of themselves as having no control over their addiction or their addictive behavior tend to give up on attempts to quit.

Here are some of the thoughts that you might have had if you've experienced the spiraling lapse:

- *One lapse means I'm a total failure.*

- *I've blown everything now! I might as well keep drinking (or using).*

- *I am hopeless.*

- *Once a drunk (or addict), always a drunk (or addict).*

- *I'll never get back to being straight again.*

- *I've screwed up today already, I might as well go all out!*

- *I have no willpower… I've lost all control.*

- *I'm just addicted to this stuff. I always will be.*

Can you think of any other thoughts you've had that are along these lines? The thoughts you'll want to identify are the ones that you tell yourself that make it more likely that you'll continue to drink or use after you've lapsed. If you can think of any that are not listed above, write them in the space provided:

_____

_____

_____

_____

Obviously, it would be best if you would get it perfectly the first time around, and never slip or lapse. But research demonstrates that relapse rates for people with addictions are similar to those for people with other chronic diseases, such as diabetes, hypertension, and asthma, occurring in 40 percent to 60 percent of those who receive treatment (McLellan 2000). What this really means is that a lapse or a relapse is *not* a sign that treatment has failed. In CBT, lapses or relapses are viewed as a sign that more treatment is needed, or that an adjustment to the treatment approach should be considered. Changes can include introducing different therapy techniques, introducing or adjusting a medication, or changing the therapy modality (such as shifting from weekly therapy to a more intensive type of program).

When it comes to the spiraling lapse, the adjustment you need may be as simple as changing your thinking about a lapse. Rather than interpreting it as a sign of failure, or the beginning of a downward spiral into relapse and loss of control, you can realize that, in the situation that triggered the lapse, you didn't cope very well. If you think of it that way, you will see that the lapse is a learning opportunity. You don't *have* to spiral into a full-blown relapse; it is *not* inevitable. If you talk about it with your counselor or therapist, and complete the exercises you'll find in the next chapter ("Step 4: Respond to Cognitive Distortions"), you can learn from your mistakes and find healthier ways to cope with similar triggering situations in the future.

Cravings

You are learning a lot about how the sequence from *trigger* to *drug or alcohol use* unfolds for you, now that you've come to understand your triggers and the thoughts they lead to. Next, we turn to the *craving* phase, which is the last experience in the sequence prior to making a decision about drinking or using. When you break the process down, and become aware of the triggers, thoughts, and cravings, then the final outcome of it (drinking or using—or *not*) does not have to be automatic. It becomes a decision that you can make with your rational brain.

Noticing all of the sensations, thoughts, and emotions that you experience during cravings is a central part of becoming a self expert. Cravings are different for everyone. The first step to beating a craving is taking a look at each of the features of the craving and understanding how you experience it. In this next exercise, you will identify how you experience cravings in your mind and body.

Exercise 5.3: How Do You Experience Cravings?

Think about the last time you had an intense craving. Now, for this first part of the exercise, try and think about where you were feeling it in your body. Put a check next to the areas or sensations below that best describe your experience.

_____   Chest (tightness or other sensation)

_____   Stomach

_____   Jaw

_____   Neck

_____   Shoulders

_____   Heart (racing)

_____   Nose (feeling like you could smell what you were craving)

_____   Other areas or sensations: _____

_____

_____

Now, try and think about the emotions you experience during a craving. Check the emotions below that best describe your experience. Add any that are not listed in the space provided at the end.

_____   Anxiety

_____   Excitement

_____   Anticipation

_____   Restlessness

_____   Irritability

_____ The same emotions I experience when I am drinking or high

_____ Other emotions: _____

_____

_____

Finally, let's identify the *cognitive* (thoughts) part of your experience. Below are some common thoughts that accompany cravings. If thoughts are a noticeable part of your experience during a craving, then place a mark next to the ones that you've experienced.

_____ *I need it.*

_____ *I have to have… (I have to have a drink).*

_____ *If I don't drink/use I'm going to go crazy.*

_____ *I can't handle… (I can't handle getting sick / the withdrawals / feeling this way).*

_____ *I can't get it out of my head.*

_____ Other thoughts: _____

_____

_____

In the next chapter, you will learn a whole new set of skills for coping with cravings. Your job right now is simply to notice everything about them.

CBT Self-Monitoring Skills

One important set of skills taught in CBT that is central to becoming a self expert is *self-monitoring* skills. Learning to self-monitor can help you to understand the psychology behind your addiction and begin to control it. By monitoring your experiences throughout each day, you become aware of your thoughts and emotions, and the behaviors that they are linked with, as they happen. Since most of us are not used to "thinking about thinking"—sometimes referred to as *metacognitive skills* (Dobson 2013)—it can be a little bit challenging at first, especially since our thoughts often go through our heads so rapidly that we don't notice them right way. But with practice, you can learn to become more self-aware, and once you do, you can start building a repertoire of CBT and other skills that you can use to change your thinking and behavior patterns in ways that support your recovery.

Exercise 5.4 provides you with a craving self-monitoring form. Using this form, you will identify your triggers, thoughts, emotions, and the intensity of your cravings. In the first column, write down the date and time of day. Next, you'll identify the situation you were in when you felt triggered. For example, did you experience an internal trigger (such as feeling depressed after an argument with your partner) or an external trigger (such as attending a party where other people were drinking or using in front of you)? Next, you will write down the thoughts that went through your mind when you were triggered and the feelings that came up for you in conjunction with your thoughts. Finally, you will rate the intensity of your craving on a scale from 0 to 10, with 0 being no cravings at all, 5 being an average number (meaning that you had some cravings but they were not constant or difficult to cope with) and 10 being severe, constant cravings.

Exercise 5.4: Craving Self-Monitoring Form

Date/Time and Triggering Situation	Thought(s)	Feelings	Craving Rating (0 to 10)

It would be helpful for you to make copies of the cravings rating form and complete it daily. (You can download the form at the website for this book, http://www .newharbinger.com/32783.) Try to fill it out in "real time" whenever you can, so that the details about your thoughts and the intensity of your cravings are as accurate as possible. By self-monitoring regularly, you may start to identify triggers and thought patterns that you weren't previously aware of that lead to cravings. By raising your awareness of your psychological experience as it relates to your addiction, you are gaining the knowledge and self-understanding that you need to be a self expert.

Wrap-up

Congratulations! You've made it through an intense set of exercises, and you are well on your way to changing your addictive behaviors. Now that you have intimate knowledge of your triggers, thoughts, and cravings, you are well positioned to learn to respond differently to the cues that used to lead you straight down a path to drinking or using. Remember to use the self-monitoring form regularly and complete all of the exercises in this chapter so that you can refer back to them as you begin practicing new coping skills. Beginning in the next chapter, you are going to develop a repertoire of skills to cope with your triggers, thoughts, and cravings without turning to alcohol or drugs.

CHAPTER 6

Step 4: Respond to Cognitive Distortions

I n the last chapter, you took a very close look at your triggers, the different types of "red flag thoughts" that enter your mind when you find yourself exposed to a trigger, and some of the errors in thinking that you are prone to making when you are tempted to drink or use. Now that you have a really thorough understanding of how triggers convert into cravings or urges, it's time to start developing a repertoire of coping skills that will enable you to get through those urges without turning to alcohol or drugs.

Just like it sounds, cognitive behavioral therapy has both *cognitive* and *behavioral* skills components. So, when you find yourself triggered or tempted to drink or use, you have two "go-to" sets of therapeutic strategies that you can choose from. In this chapter, you will learn to use both of these types of skills to cope with the distorted thoughts that you experience when you are triggered. As you practice these new skills, pay special attention to which ones are the most useful to you, as well as which ones don't work quite as well. From this chapter forward, based on your own observations and reflections about your experiences trying out these different techniques, you will start forming your individualized relapse prevention plan.

Outsmarting Your Addicted Brain

We've talked about your addicted brain and how the exercises in this workbook will help you "defeat it" by making your rational brain stronger. That's what the *cognitive* part of CBT is all about. The red flag thoughts you identified in chapter 5 are the byproducts of your addicted brain. This is the part of you that finds ways of justifying a relapse to feed those uncomfortable urges. With practice, you can challenge these thoughts successfully and "outsmart" your lower, addicted brain. When you do that repeatedly, your rational mindset will start to become the new normal for you, and you can begin to break free from the thoughts that have been interfering with the goals you've set for your recovery.

Thought Challenging

As you learn to outsmart your addicted brain, the most powerful cognitive technique you will use is the skill of *thought challenging*. As you practice this method of transforming irrational thinking into balanced, realistic thoughts, you will learn to take a scientific approach to correcting the thoughts that are leading you down a path to self-destructive behaviors, like drinking and using drugs.

One of the most important things you will get out of learning CBT techniques like thought challenging is something that applies not only to overcoming addiction, but also to coping with other problems that stem from irrational thoughts (like depression, anxiety, and other emotional difficulties). You will learn to understand and change your behavior by being scientific, and sticking to the facts. *What does that mean, exactly?* you might be wondering. *How can I be "scientific"?* It's not as complicated as it might sound, actually. You can achieve this by learning to notice and respond to your thoughts in several ways.

1. First, to become scientific, you need to practice *observing* yourself. You are already making headway toward becoming an objective observer of your experience, having begun to monitor your thoughts and cravings, and identify your mistakes in thinking.

2. Next, you'll need to practice *questioning* whether your thoughts are rational—especially the ones that relate to drinking or using drugs. Thought challenging is the process of questioning your thoughts about drinking and using by asking yourself if you have *evidence* that they are true.

3. Finally, after you question the evidence for your thoughts, if you find that you *don't* have evidence to support what you are thinking, then you will identify more rational, evidence-based ideas that you can tell yourself instead. These new, healthy and balanced thoughts will help you make the behavior changes you set out to accomplish in your recovery plan.

To put the thought challenging process into action, you're going to need a framework. First, we'll take a look at a few examples of how to challenge common red flag thoughts. Once you get the hang of it, you can complete the worksheet using your own examples. This worksheet can be used to review patterns of thinking that have led you to drink or use in the past. And if you slip or relapse at any time in the future, the exercises can help you (and your treatment provider, if you have one) to understand how the relapse unfolded and what you can do differently going forward.

Scott Gets Triggered

Scott has a strong urge to drink a glass of wine. On a scale from 0 to 10, he rates his craving as a 7. He thinks about it and realizes that it is because he is at a party with some friends he used to drink with.

Scott can try thought challenging by following three steps, which we will call the three T's: identifying the **t**riggering situation, and the red flag **t**houghts about drinking or using that followed, and placing the thoughts on **t**rial:

Triggering situation: Hanging out with drinking buddies at a party

Red flag thoughts: *If I have just one drink, it's no big deal. I can control it.*

Thoughts on trial: Scott puts his thoughts on trial by *examining the evidence* for them. Below you will find the questions he asks to figure out whether his addicted brain is driving the thoughts or if they are rational, and the *honest* answers he comes up with.

Questions to Ask to Examine the Evidence	The Facts
Is one drink okay?	*Yes. Having one drink is not destructive.*
Can I control my drinking enough to stop after one drink?	*It's been too long to even remember the last time I stopped after one drink. The likelihood of that is extremely low.*

Result: Now that Scott has used the three T's to challenge his thoughts, it's time for him to take a look at the result, and take action accordingly. In this example, as a result of the thought challenging exercise, Scott can see that his thought about having one drink was irrational. Although it is true that one drink is not harmful to most people, when he takes an honest look at his past patterns of behavior, he can recognize that there is no good evidence that he can control his drinking in the way that he wishes to. Even though he might be able to have one drink from time to time, before long it would likely lead him back to his older patterns of drinking heavily. The idea that he could have "just one drink" is exactly the kind of thought that the addicted brain produces to feed the urge to drink.

Response: Okay, so Scott had an irrational thought. We all experience irrational thoughts, whether they are about drinking or something else. The important question that follows is, how can you respond to it? When you respond, your goal is to get your mind back on track, to line it back up with your recovery—and of course, with reality! To do this, Scott can respond by telling himself the following:

- *For me, one drink is a big deal. In the past, this way of thinking has led me straight to a full-blown relapse.*

- *There is plenty of evidence that I practically never stop after one drink, and I am not able to control myself once I start drinking.*

Lucy Gets Triggered

Lucy has a strong urge to use cocaine. On a scale from 0 to 10, she rates her craving as an 8. She thinks about it and realizes that it is because she is feeling depressed and low in energy, and she's looking for something to "pick her up."

Lucy tries thought challenging, using the three T's:

Triggering situation: Feeling depressed and low in energy

Red flag thoughts: *Cocaine is the only thing that will make me feel better. It will help me get stuff done.*

Thoughts on trial: Lucy puts her thoughts on trial as she *examines the evidence* for them:

Questions to Ask to Examine the Evidence	The Facts
Will cocaine make me feel better?	*At first, yes, it will. But when it wears off, I will be even more depressed, and I will feel bad about having caved in and used.*
Is cocaine the only thing that will make me feel better?	*Probably not. There are healthier things that could make me feel better—like talking to someone, or exercising, or doing something fun.*
Will cocaine help me get stuff done?	*At first, yes, I will have more energy to get stuff done. But there are only so many things I can do well if I'm high. And then when I crash afterward, I might not get anything done for days.*

Result: Now that Lucy has used the three T's to challenge her thoughts, she can see that her thoughts about using cocaine to feel better and get things done was irrational. Although there is some superficial truth to the idea that using cocaine could lift her mood in the moment, and help her to get some extra energy, when she takes a more thorough and honest look at the evidence, she realizes that the longer-term impact of using, over the days and hours that follow, would counteract all of the positives that would come of it.

Response: To get herself back into her recovering mindset, Lucy can respond by telling herself the following:

- *Cocaine makes my depression worse, not better. Even though I might feel good for a short time, using always makes me more depressed once it's over.*

- *There is plenty of evidence that when I use, I am less productive. I get depressed and barely do anything for days afterward.*

- *Just because I get more energy for a short time doesn't mean that using is going to lead me to get a lot of stuff done.*

Brian Gets Triggered

Brian has a craving to use marijuana. On a scale from 0 to 10, he rates his craving as a 7. Upon reflection, he realizes that it's because he is nervous about going to a party by himself, and he'd like to smoke some pot to take the edge off.

Brian tries thought challenging, using the three T's:

Triggering situation: Going to a party alone and feeling some social anxiety about it

Red flag thoughts: *If I'm high, I won't feel so self-conscious and it won't be as hard to talk to people.*

Thoughts on trial: Brian puts his thoughts on trial as he *examines the evidence* that marijuana will help him feel and socialize better at the party.

Questions to Ask to Examine the Evidence	The Facts
Will marijuana take the edge off and make me feel better?	*At first, yes, it will. But when it wears off, my mood will be down, and I won't feel so great for a day or two.*
Will being high help me handle myself better at the party?	*Not entirely. I won't feel as self-conscious, so it will be easier to be there alone. But usually when I am high I'm a little distant and I don't really connect well with new people.*
Is it worth it to use marijuana in this situation?	*It will make me feel better in the moment, but I probably won't socialize very much at the party. And because of the effect it will have on my mood and energy afterward, it's not worth it.*

Result: Now that Brian has used the three T's to take a closer look at his thoughts about using marijuana to cope with his anxiety, he can see that, on balance, his thoughts were irrational. Although there is some superficial truth to the idea that getting high can reduce his social anxiety, when he takes an honest survey of the evidence, he concludes that the negative effects of smoking marijuana outweigh the benefits. He asks himself an important question to conclude his thought challenging exercise: Is it worth it to use in this situation? This is a question that you can use to make a decision about what to do when the results of your thought challenging are not crystal clear. In Brian's case, marijuana use has some beneficial effects on his social anxiety, so balancing the positive and negative outcomes of using was a helpful way of making a rational decision.

Response: To weigh the evidence for his decision about marijuana use more rationally, Brian can respond by telling himself the following:

- *Getting high makes me a little awkward and distant in social situations. Even though I might feel less self-conscious, I won't really connect with anyone at the party. In that case, there's not much point in going if I have to get high to get myself there.*

- *There is plenty of evidence that when I use, it affects my mood negatively and I don't function so well for a day or two.*

- *Just because I won't feel so self-conscious doesn't mean that using is worth it.*

Superficial Truths: Watch Out for Them!

You might have noticed that in both Brian and Lucy's examples, they were tempted to use by certain thoughts that turned out to be *superficial truths*. That means that some short-term benefit of drinking or using gives the decision to slip or relapse some major appeal. This can get somewhat confusing—because it is a rational element of your thought process about drinking and using. It *does* feel good at first. That's true. It *can* relieve anxiety in the short-term. That's true. If you really think about it, you will find that it makes sense that there are *some* positive effects that drinking or using drugs has on you—otherwise you wouldn't have found yourself doing more of it in the first place!

The key is to consider those positives in the bigger context of why you're trying to quit. Yes, it feels good at first in certain situations, but *then* what happens? What is it about the sequence that starts with feeling good that led you to pick up this book and work so hard to stop? One of the goals of thought challenging is to be able to recognize when you are allowing yourself to be persuaded to make choices about drinking or using by superficial truths, and challenge them.

Exercise 6.1: Thought Challenging Worksheet

Use this worksheet to challenge the evidence for your red flag thoughts using the three T's.

Triggering situation: _____

_____

Red flag thoughts: _____

_____

Thought on trial: _____

_____

Evidence that the thoughts are accurate:

_____

_____

_____

_____

Evidence that the thoughts are superficial truths or not accurate:

_____

_____

_____

_____

Response (What can you tell yourself to get back into the recovery mindset?):

_____

_____

_____

Responding to the Most Common Thought Errors

In chapter 5, you learned about different kinds of mistakes in thinking that can lead to red flag thoughts. Before you continue to practice thought challenging using the errors in thinking that you wrote down on the Thought Challenging Worksheet, take a look at the table that follows for some suggestions about how to respond to the most common mistakes in thinking. Remember, the first thing to do once you recognize that you've made one of the thought errors below is to make yourself aware of it by starting an internal dialogue about what just happened. (*Okay, wait a minute. I'm starting to do that black-or-white thinking again…*) Then, once you have become aware of it, you can use the three T's and respond to your thought error using the kinds of thoughts or responses you see in the right hand column of the table below.

Thought Error	Red Flag Thoughts	Response
Black-or-white thought	*I messed up everything at work; I might as well drink.*	*I didn't mess up everything. Everyone makes mistakes sometimes. Drinking won't fix it; it will make everything worse.*
Discounting the positive	*My boss only said something nice to me out of pity. I'm pathetic; I have nothing to lose by drinking.*	*Just because I made a mistake at work doesn't mean that all of the positive things my boss says to me are untrue. I have a lot to lose by drinking; it can only make things more problematic at work. That's why I decided to get into recovery.*
Jumping to conclusions	*With my luck treatment won't work for me. I'll never stay clean and sober. There's no point in trying.*	*I won't know if treatment works until I try it and gather some evidence. If it's not working, then I can figure out what other options I have.*
Taking your feelings too seriously	*I feel hopeless; therefore my life must be hopeless. I might as well use.*	*Just because I feel a certain way doesn't make it a reality. Feelings can and do change. Using won't change my life situation, but working on myself will.*
Self-blame	*It's all my fault that I drink too much. I've ruined my life.*	*I have a disease, and I am taking positive steps to recover. It won't happen overnight, but I can turn things around if I stay clean and sober.*
Labeling	*I drink too much. I'm just a loser.*	*Having an illness doesn't make me a loser. If I take care of myself and my condition, I can recover.*
Spiraling Lapse	*I've already screwed up today by drinking; I might as well go all out!*	*The way I respond to a slip can make all the difference in my recovery. I don't have to screw up the whole day. If I stop now, I can stay on the path to recovery. Every decision I make about drinking is important.*

Exercise 6.2: Challenging Your Red Flag Thoughts

Now that you have some examples to work from, try the thought-challenging exercise again, using one of the thoughts that you wrote down in chapter 5, when you identified your most common mistakes in thinking. In this exercise, we'll assume that you already know what the trigger is, and you are making yourself aware of the thought error you're making.

Red flag thoughts: _____

Thoughts on trial: _____

Evidence that the thoughts are accurate: _____

_____

_____

Evidence that the thoughts are superficial truths or not accurate: _____

_____

_____

_____

Response (What can you tell yourself to get back into the recovery mindset?):

_____

_____

_____

Now that you've had some practice with thought challenging, you can build on the self-monitoring skills you learned in chapter 5, adding on the exercise of challenging red flag thoughts after you notice them. Practice completing the worksheet that follows (also available at http://www.newharbinger.com/32783) on a daily basis, any time you get triggered. You can review your entries with your counselor or therapist (if you have one) as part of your treatment.

Thinking vs. Doing

Some people can change their behavior by thinking their way through their irrational brain's ideas, challenging them, and converting them into healthy, rational thoughts. Sometimes, and for some people, rather than correcting red flag thoughts using *cognitive* techniques like thought challenging, it works better to change what they're *doing*, using *behavioral* coping strategies. There are a few reasons why that might be. For some, it has to do with the timing in recovery. That is, in early recovery, when cravings for alcohol and drugs can be very strong and emotions can be overwhelming, it might be hard to concentrate or think clearly enough to have the inner dialogue that thought challenging requires. For others, it's just a general preference for getting out of their own head. They may find it an easier way of preventing relapse than using a cognitive strategy.

Surf the Urge

The average length of a craving is about fifteen minutes. Even though that can feel like a lifetime when you're so uncomfortable physically and emotionally, you might find it helpful to keep it in perspective and remember that it *will* end! For some people, it's useful to imagine the craving as a wave in the ocean—it will climb until it peaks, and then it will crash and subside. If you can get through that brief period of time by riding it out, the discomfort will pass, and your recovery will grow stronger. As you are riding the urge out, you will experience the urge sensations weakening and going away. The goal is to ride it out without reacting to it by drinking or using. You will learn more about how to use similar techniques to this one in the next chapter, on becoming mindful.

Exercise 6.3: Thought Challenging Form

Triggering Situation	Red Flag Thoughts	Thoughts on Trial (Questions I asked myself to examine the evidence)	→	Alternative Responses

Distract Yourself

Have you ever noticed, when you experience an urge to drink or use, that the longer you spend thinking about it, the harder it is to resist it? This is a very common experience, so if you've had it, you are not alone. In a way, thinking about drinking or using is like entertaining a fantasy, and the more invested you are in imagining how it will play out, the more you want it. The more you want it, the less you are able to weigh the pros and cons and make a rational decision about it. With this knowledge, you can choose to distract yourself from the urge before your imagination runs away with it and leads you to a relapse. Here are some ways that you can distract yourself early on, when you first notice the urge:

- Imagine a big, red STOP sign as soon as you feel the urge. Hold that image in your mind for as long as you can.

- Wear a rubber band around your wrist. If you feel an urge, snap it just to distract your attention from it.

- If you can, leave the situation that triggered the urge.

- Go for a walk or engage in another form of exercise.

- Find a distracting activity that can hold your attention for fifteen or twenty minutes, whether it's writing, reading, going somewhere that feels safe, or calling someone.

- Meditate or use other relaxation exercises. (You will learn more about how to do this in the next chapter.)

- Pray.

- Go to a 12-step or other self-help meeting. You can download an app, such as The Meeting Finder, onto your phone that will locate the closest meeting to you at any time.

- Talk to somebody who supports your recovery. This can be a friend, therapist, 12-step sponsor, or family member. Just talking to somebody can help you get through a tough moment, whether you talk about the urge or craving itself or a completely different topic.

- Use imagery to get your mind to a different place. You can try imagining a safe, quiet place, or a place that you would love to be in that moment. Just be sure that the place you choose is not compatible with drinking or using.

Start experimenting with these distraction techniques and see what works for you. We'll put them into your personalized relapse prevention plan later. If you think of some distracting activities not listed here that are helpful to you, list them here:

_____

_____

_____

_____

Delay the Decision

Now that you have some ideas about how to distract yourself from an urge or craving, you can use these distractions to *delay the decision* about whether or not to drink or use for at least fifteen or twenty minutes. This can be a very useful way to fight off the impulse to give in to an urge, which usually lasts only fifteen or twenty minutes. You'll find, more often than not, that once you've made it through that initial period of time and the urge has subsided, it is easier to make a firm commitment to not drink or use. If you are still uncertain after fifteen or twenty minutes, repeat the exercise: distract yourself and delay the decision for another fifteen or twenty minutes.

Keep a Schedule

Although red flag thoughts and cravings are very common, especially when you first quit or cut back on drinking or using drugs, there are ways that you can prevent them from coming on in the first place. When you became a self expert in chapter 5, you learned how to identify your triggers. One way to build on this skill is to schedule how you will spend your days in advance, so you can anticipate when you might find yourself in a triggering situation, and plan for it. Consider an example:

Scott's schedule for Monday is as follows:

7:00 a.m.: Wake up; eat breakfast

8:00 a.m.: Take kids to school

9:00 a.m.: Arrive at work

11:30 a.m.: Meeting with boss**

12:00 p.m.: Lunch hour**

5:00 p.m.: Leave work

6:00 p.m.: Make dinner

6:30–7:30 p.m.: Dinner, winding down the evening

7:30–9:30 p.m.: Free time (kids asleep)**

9:30 p.m.–bedtime: Wife gets home from work; spend time together

**High-risk or triggering situations

By writing out his schedule, Scott identified three potentially triggering situations: First, he has been having some difficulties at work, and he gets very stressed when he meets with his boss, which has triggered cravings and urges for him in the past. His meeting with his boss on Monday is just before lunch hour, and since he doesn't have any lunch meetings, Scott might be tempted to go out for lunch and have a glass of wine with his meal—lunch hour was often the time when he had his first drink of the day. Another risky time for him is when he is alone. After putting his kids to bed at 7:30, he can anticipate experiencing an urge to drink while waiting for his wife to get home from her late shift at work.

Scott will need to plan out what he will do at each of these risky times. The key, however, is that he was able to identify them in advance because he wrote out his schedule. Finding an effective coping strategy is easiest to do when you've planned for it. To practice this, use the daily schedule that follows. Once we've reviewed some more behavioral coping skills that you can use during these risky times, you will start using the Urge Planner (exercise 6.5) to plan ahead for them.

Exercise 6.4: Daily Schedule

When you complete your daily schedule, try to fill in as much as you can, including what time you wake up, shower, eat, exercise, and work; any appointments you have; social or family plans; errands; and anything else you are able to think of. As you begin to keep a detailed schedule, notice which planned activities might be triggering for you and place asterisks (**) next to them. It will also help to pay attention to blocks of time in your day when you might not have anything planned; these, for some people, are vulnerable times when cravings or urges often come up. By noticing and paying special attention to these high-risk times, you can start to structure your time more, as needed, with activities that are not compatible with drinking or using (for example, going to a 12-step or other recovery-oriented meeting, or spending time with a sober friend or loved one).

Date: _____

7:00 a.m. _____

8:00 a.m. _____

9:00 a.m. _____

10:00 a.m. _____

11:00 a.m. _____

12:00 p.m. _____

1:00 p.m. _____

2:00 p.m. _____

3:00 p.m. _____

4:00 p.m. _____

5:00 p.m. _____

6:00 p.m. _____

7:00 p.m. _____

8:00 p.m. _____

9:00 p.m. _____

10:00 p.m. _____

11:00 p.m. _____

12:00 a.m. _____

Planning for High-Risk Situations

A *high-risk situation* is any situation that might be triggering for you. While scheduling your time can help you to avoid high-risk situations, some are unavoidable—for example, stressful interactions with coworkers or family members, obligatory work functions where others might be drinking, or any experience that brings up unpleasant emotions. Like Scott, you can plan for upcoming high-risk situations by thinking ahead of time about how you can handle them.

Let's take one of Scott's anticipated urges as an example. Scott has a meeting scheduled with his boss just before his lunch hour. Those meetings are always stressful, and Scott anticipates that he will be tempted to go out to lunch by himself afterward and drink a glass of wine.

To be ready to cope with this situation, Scott needs to have at least two ideas: a plan and a backup plan. These are the plans he comes up with:

Plan: Make lunch plans with a friend from work, Bianca, whom I wouldn't drink with during work hours.

Backup plan: Bring lunch to eat at my desk, and schedule a call with my AA sponsor for that time, so he can help me if I'm feeling triggered.

Now it's your turn to use the Urge Planner for any high-risk situations you might have identified in your schedule for the upcoming week.

Exercise 6.5: Urge Planner

What situations do you anticipate this week that will trigger urges to drink or use?

High-risk situation #1 (include day, time, and situation): _____

_____

How can you plan to cope with the urges?

Plan: _____

Backup plans: (1) _____

(2) _____

High-risk situation #2 (include day, time, and situation): _____

_____

How can you plan to cope with the urges?

Plan: _____

Backup plans: (1) _____

(2) _____

High-risk situation #3 (include day, time, and situation): _____

_____

How can you plan to cope with the urges?

Plan: _____

Backup plans: (1) _____

(2) _____

Are you someone who gets more out of cognitive strategies than behavioral ones, or vice versa? Are both types of skills helpful to you? Does it depend on the situation? As you are developing your personal relapse prevention plan, you'll want to ask yourself these questions. If this workbook is your first exposure to CBT, then you are still in the process of gathering evidence to answer those questions. As you continue your cognitive and behavioral coping skills practice, give some thought to which ones work for you best, so that you can emphasize them when you make your relapse prevention plan in chapter 10.

Wrap-up

In this chapter, you've started to form a repertoire of skills to cope with your triggers, thoughts, and cravings without turning to alcohol or drugs. You've learned cognitive skills, such as identifying red flag thoughts and superficial truths and challenging them. You've also been practicing behavioral skills, which include distracting yourself and keeping a schedule. The best way for you to begin to develop a relapse prevention plan that works for you is to continue to practice these techniques week after week (including making use of the Urge Planner, the daily schedule, and the thought challenging form), and make notes in your workbook about the ones that you have found to be the most helpful.

All of these skills require practice before using them will come naturally to you in a risky situation, so the more you work on them, the better. And don't be too hard on yourself if it doesn't always occur to you to use them. Just as it took a while for your use of alcohol or drugs to form an addiction, it will also take some time for you to learn new ways of responding to your urges to drink or use. Be patient with yourself.

In the next chapter, you will learn a different, equally useful approach to dealing with uncomfortable cravings or urges: rather than trying to change your thoughts or distract yourself from them, you are going to practice accepting and exploring them.

CHAPTER 7

Step 5: Become Mindful

Now that you are getting a lot of practice with the **C** of CBT skills (that is, the cognitive part), you are becoming more and more skillful at identifying mistakes in thinking, challenging them, and coming up with healthier alternatives that lead you away from drinking and using. In this chapter, you will learn a new set of skills to complement those cognitive therapy techniques.

Remember how we talked about the fact that sometimes it's hard to *think* your way through an uncomfortable moment when you're having a craving? Cognitive techniques like thought challenging can be difficult to use at times, especially when the craving feels very powerful, or you can't clear your head, or you're too overwhelmed to come up with healthier thoughts to replace the irrational ones. Mindfulness skills can be very helpful to you in a moment like that. When you use mindfulness techniques, rather than trying to *change* what you're thinking, or come up with alternatives, you learn to accept and tolerate unpleasant thoughts or experiences (such as cravings) without drinking or using in response to them.

The purpose of this chapter is to give you a basic understanding of what mindfulness is, to show you how mindfulness techniques and meditation can be helpful to you in your recovery, and to give you some practice exercises so that you can familiarize yourself with how to use them.

What Is Mindfulness?

Mindfulness, one of the most widely used and studied forms of meditation, was first introduced to Western psychology by Dr. Jon Kabat-Zinn at the University of Massachusetts Medical School (Kabat-Zinn 1990). He developed an eight-week program called mindfulness-based stress reduction, originally to help people with chronic pain; from there, the treatment was extended to individuals suffering from anxiety and depression (Kabat-Zinn et al. 1992; Roemer and Orsillo 2003; Ramel et al. 2004; Evans et al. 2008) and cancer (Carlson et al. 2004), and finally to normal, healthy adults struggling with stress (Astin 1997; Shapiro, Schwartz, and Bonner 1998; Williams et al. 2001).

If you're not experienced with meditation, you are probably wondering what mindfulness is, exactly. Mindfulness is defined as "awareness that emerges through paying attention, on purpose, in the present moment, and non-judgmentally to the unfolding of experience, moment by moment." (Kabat-Zinn 2003, 145). Let's take a look at what that means:

- *Awareness:* We all have habits or ways of behaving that we've been doing the same way for so long that we don't even notice when they are happening. Drinking or using in response to certain triggers (like stress or negative feelings) can be one of those habits. When you learn to be mindful, you become *aware* of the sequence of experiences you have that lead you to drink or use, before it actually happens. There are many parts of your experience that you can learn to be aware of, including the physical sensations throughout your body, your breathing, your thoughts, your intentions, and your emotions.

- *...that emerges through paying attention, on purpose, in the present moment:* Our attention naturally wanders from one thing to another. We are often distracted from something we are paying attention to by our own thoughts or feelings or things that are happening in our environment. One of the ways to learn to be aware of our experience in the here and now is to become purposefully attentive to it. That often means recognizing when something has distracted us, and purposely redirecting our attention to the here and now experience. In recovery, paying attention, on purpose, to the experience of a craving or a negative feeling can help you to learn more about yourself and your addiction, and to find your way through the craving or negative emotion without trying to run away from it by drinking or using.

- *...nonjudgmentally:* Whatever our experience is, we are used to labeling things. Do you ever find yourself saying to yourself when you feel upset, something like, *I shouldn't feel upset*? If so, you are not the only one who does that; it's what minds naturally do. We often judge our experience; we label it as good or bad, justified or unjustified, given the circumstances. When you experience an urge to drink or use, maybe you judge it, feel guilty about it, or wish that it weren't there. It comes very naturally—partly as a way of making sense of our experience and our world—to label, evaluate, or otherwise judge what we feel. When you practice mindfulness, you reserve those judgments, accepting each aspect of your experience just the way it is. An important part of this is bringing a gentle kindness to your experience, as a way of showing compassion to yourself. As you probably already know, recovery has a lot of uncomfortable moments. Paying attention to those moments on purpose, with compassion and without judging yourself for them, is one powerful way to find your way through them.

- *...to the unfolding of experience, moment by moment:* Our experiences are all temporary. Feelings change, thoughts come in and out of our minds, and physical sensations come and go. We can't predict how our experiences are going to change from one moment to the next, but when practicing mindfulness, we can observe the way our thoughts, emotions, and bodily sensations unfold, and learn about them with open curiosity. As you get better at becoming an *observer* of your experience without *reacting* to it in the moment, you will gain better control over the way that you cope with difficult experiences.

Why Mindfulness?

Now that you have a good sense of what mindfulness is, you are probably wondering how it can be useful for addiction. It is only in very recent years that this approach has been adapted specifically to help people with addictions, based on several known facts about mindfulness and drug and alcohol problems:

- Mindfulness is very helpful for managing stress, which is one of the most common triggers for relapse to alcohol and drug use (Hanson 2002; Sinha 2007, 2008; Tate et al. 2008).

- Heavy use of alcohol or drugs can cause damage to certain areas of the brain that enable you to think of a healthy way to cope with stress when you are confronted with it in the moment. These are areas of the brain that help you think through possible ways to manage a problem or stressor, and at the same time control your impulse to use unhealthy coping strategies that will give you a "quick fix"—like drinking or using drugs (Sinha 2008).

- Mindfulness can help you retrain your brain to take a thoughtful approach to *respond* to the stress, rather than *reacting* to it impulsively by using alcohol or drugs, or engaging in other self-destructive behaviors.

- Studies show that practicing mindfulness helps relieve depression and anxiety, which are two of the most common psychological symptoms that are experienced by people with addictions (Glasner-Edwards et al. 2009; Breslin, Zack, and McMain 2002; Marlatt, 1996). Like stress, these symptoms often lead to relapse, so by learning to manage them, you increase your chances of long-term recovery. In fact, a recent study proved this pattern exactly: adults with drug addiction who received mindfulness training showed improvements in symptoms of depression and anxiety, and learning mindfulness techniques for recovery was especially useful to addicts with diagnosed depression and anxiety, in improving their substance use (Glasner-Edwards et al., forthcoming).

- Studies show that practicing mindfulness reduces cravings for alcohol and drugs (Witkiewitz, Lustyk, and Bowen 2013) and is helpful to people who are in recovery from addictions in preventing relapse (Bowen et al. 2014).

Getting Started: Being Present

When you get out of bed in the morning and start getting ready to begin your day, is your mind in the present, or is it off somewhere else? Here's an example of how you'd know: When you're brushing your teeth in the morning, are you paying attention to the way that the bristles feel as they circle around against your teeth, or the minty sensation of the toothpaste in your mouth? Chances are, the answer is no. When you brush your teeth, your mind is probably doing what minds naturally do—they plan and anticipate what's to come, and when they are not jumping into the future, they are reviewing past experiences. So you might be thinking about the day ahead of you, reminding yourself what time your first commitment starts, or planning how you are going to approach a meeting or interaction you know you are going to have that day. Maybe you're reviewing something that happened yesterday or last week, playing a tape of it back in your mind.

This "mode" of doing things without being present as you do them, is called *automatic pilot* (Bowen, Chawla, and Marlatt 2010). You can do a lot of things in automatic pilot mode, especially things that you do every day. Certain elements of your daily routine (like brushing your teeth, taking a shower, eating breakfast, or driving to work or school) are so well rehearsed, that you don't need to think about them as you are doing them. Your mind feels free to wander, and it makes its way into the past or the future. When you learn mindfulness skills, you *purposely* keep your mind in the here and now, gently bringing it back to the present whenever it wanders off.

What does this have to do with addiction? you might be wondering. The concept of automatic pilot is actually very relevant to addiction, and here's how: Over time, addictive behaviors become like habits. Have you ever found yourself drinking or using without being completely aware of how or why you started? It's something you've probably done many times without really thinking about it, or without any *awareness* that there were thoughts, emotions, and possibly physical sensations that led up to it (Marlatt and Ostafin 2005). As you learn to become more connected to your experience in the present, you can begin to make a shift from reacting automatically and out of habit to your thoughts and feelings to making *mindful* choices about your behavior (especially those that involve drugs and alcohol) with kindness and self-compassion. These mindful choices about drinking and using become available to you when you are *tuned in* and *aware* of your urges and cravings as they occur.

To begin to step out of automatic pilot, you are going to be introduced to a series of exercises. When you practice the principles of mindfulness, try not to judge yourself. If you are new to mindfulness or to meditation in general, the exercises may seem a little awkward. You may find yourself wondering whether or not you're doing them right. Remember that there is no right or wrong when you are practicing mindfulness; you are simply learning to observe your experience. Whether the experience feels good, bad, strange, or neutral, you will simply observe it, bringing your mind gently and kindly back to it whenever it wanders (and it will, because all minds do!). This is a skill that takes practice, so try to be patient. You'll get the hang of it with time.

Exercise 7.1: Observe Your Body

To become an observer of your experience, you will first need a little bit of practice with the skill of observing. In this first exercise, you are going to practice observing your body, or your physical self. Keep in mind that this exercise is not intended to make you feel a certain way; it is not a relaxation exercise, but rather an exercise in observation. What you are practicing here is becoming present and aware of your physical body, whether that feels relaxing, neutral, or even uncomfortable. Just observe it, whatever it is.

Begin by sitting in a comfortable position, taking a moment to notice the movement of your breath, the rising and the falling of your chest with each inhale and exhale. Stay with your breath in this way for a minute. When you're ready, bring your awareness to the physical sensations in your body, beginning with the sensations of your body making contact with your chair, and your feet making contact with the ground. Just take a moment to observe how that feels. If you're feeling restless, or distracted by thoughts, sounds, or things that you can see in your environment, just congratulate yourself for noticing that your mind has wandered, and gently bring yourself back to awareness of your body.

Now bring your awareness to your feet. Notice any sensations you have in your feet, paying attention to their temperature, the way their contact with your shoes (if you're wearing any) feels, the sensations of the toes touching each other, and any sensations on the sole, top of the foot, and ankle.

Moving away from the feet, bring your awareness to your legs. Use your awareness of your legs to explore every sensation there, beginning with anything you feel in your calves, your knees, and your thighs. Pay attention to the areas of your legs that make contact with your chair, noticing the sensations there.

Now gently guide your awareness to your hips and waist. If you observe any pain or discomfort, just practice being aware of it and letting it be as it is. Moving your awareness to your back, begin with your lower back and bring your attention to any sensations there. Now move to your upper back, paying attention to where your back makes contact with your chair. Notice any tension or discomfort.

Next, guide your attention to your arms. Beginning at your hands and moving upward, bring your awareness to any sensations you feel in your wrists, forearms, elbows, upper arms, and finally, shoulders. Now focus your attention on your neck. Notice any tension there. Moving up the neck, begin exploring the sensations on your face. Bring your attention to the sensations you feel on your forehead, eyelids, eyebrows, nose, and cheeks.

Moving to your lips, bring your attention to your jaw and chin. Just notice any sensations there. Then bring your awareness to the very top of your head. Now that you've explored the sensations in the various parts of your body, just take a few moments to experience your body as a whole, connecting again with your breath as you did when you began this exercise.

The intention behind doing exercises like this, that teach you to use mindful awareness when paying attention to your body, is to help you learn the skill of being present. It sounds simple, but it takes a tremendous amount of practice for most people to get comfortable with this. When doing any mindfulness meditation practice, try and remember to approach it with these few points in mind (which were reviewed earlier, but you are reminded of them here for emphasis):

- This exercise is not intended to help you relax or have a certain kind of new experience within your body. Try to let go of any expectations about how this exercise will feel, and just let it be whatever it is. Remember that the purpose of the exercise is to be present and aware of whatever your experience is.

- If you get distracted, or you feel strange doing the exercise, or if you like or dislike it, just notice those aspects of your experience and gently bring your attention back to the exercise.

- Be open and curious about your experience, without judging or trying to change it. Practice accepting your experience just the way that it is. You can even try telling yourself, *This is just the way things are right now.* This can be helpful to you when you are practicing the exercise itself or when you are using mindfulness in your daily life, to cope with uncomfortable emotions, urges, cravings, or other experiences that you may find stressful or difficult.

Living Mindfully

Daily life is full of opportunities to practice mindfulness, without a workbook in front of you. Think about all of the things that you do automatically, without thinking. Take driving, for example. When you are driving your car, do you pay attention to what your foot feels like when it makes contact with the gas pedal, or when it shifts from the gas pedal to the brake? Are you aware of the coordination between your hands on the steering wheel and the continuous movements of your feet, integrating your mind's intentions to head straight or turn right, and slow down or speed up at the same time? If you're like most people, the answer to these questions is "no." When you're driving, you are probably planning what you are going to do when you arrive at your destination, or what you'll be doing later that day. Maybe your mind fast-forwards to the weekend, and what you have planned. Maybe you think about things that you are worried about. Or maybe you are talking on the phone as you drive, and it's that conversation that occupies your mind's space.

Driving is just one example of things that we can do easily in automatic pilot mode. Other things we do without being present include eating, bathing, washing our hands, and walking. In this next exercise, you are going to try a few of these daily activities with mindful awareness.

Exercise 7.2: Bringing Mindfulness Practice into Your Daily Life

Practice being present and aware as you do each of the activities below. As you pay attention to your experience, notice how your mind naturally wanders away from the activity and gently bring it back to the present moment.

After you complete each exercise, ask yourself some questions about it: What did you experience? What did you notice? Were there sensations (physical sensations, feelings, smells, or other sensations) that you were not aware of before you approached the activity in this way? What were they? Jot down some of your observations in the space provided after each exercise.

Take a Mindful Shower

The mindful shower is a nice way to begin your day with awareness. This could set the tone for your entire day, helping you to notice when you are in automatic pilot so that you can purposely shift your attention to the present moment.

Begin by slowly setting your right foot into the shower, paying attention to the sensation of your foot making contact with the floor. Transferring the weight of your body entirely to your right foot and leg, notice, as you lift your left foot and move it forward to join your right foot on the shower floor, the sensations in your left leg as it rises into the air, and in your left foot as it makes contact with the floor. Notice your body's stability in this standing position.

As you turn on the shower, move the dial slowly, paying attention to the way your hand grasps the dial, and the intention with which it moves the dial to the position that turns it on and adjusts it to your preference. Guide your attention to the sensations you feel on your skin as the droplets of water make contact with it. Pay attention to the temperature of the water and how the temperature of your skin changes as the water touches it.

Next, spend a few moments guiding your awareness to the sounds that you hear as the water emerges from the showerhead and makes contact with your body. If you find that your mind is wandering, worrying, planning, reviewing, or thinking about anything else, congratulate yourself for noticing this and guide your awareness back to the present moment, in the shower.

Notice any smells. Maybe the soap has a familiar smell. Spend a few moments guiding your attention to anything you can smell.

After you get out of the shower, see if you can continue your routine of getting ready with this mindful approach. Then make some notes about your experience.

My observations during my mindful shower: _____

_____

_____

_____

_____

Eat Mindfully

In this exercise, you will pay attention to your experience of eating, moment by moment. Try it with a piece of fruit—an apple, orange, or banana. When you try this for the first time, remember that it will be just you having a few minutes with the fruit, so keep the television and radio off, and try to minimize sources of distraction.

First, without holding it yet, take a look at the fruit as though you've never seen it before. Notice its shape, its color, and any other features that you can see. Pay attention to whether it needs to be peeled to be eaten. After you've taken in its appearance, pick up the fruit and look at it more closely. Notice if your mind wanders or if you find yourself making any judgments about the activity itself. When this happens, be kind to yourself, gently bringing your attention back to the fruit.

Next, bring the fruit to your ear to see if it makes any sounds. Gently acknowledge any impatience or other feelings that come up during the exercise, bringing your attention back to the fruit each time. Now bring the fruit near to your nose, observing whether you are able to smell it, and if so, how it smells—whether the smell is familiar, sweet, sour, or neutral.

As you prepare to take a bite, bring it slowly to your mouth, but before your mouth makes contact, notice how it is preparing to receive the fruit. Notice whether saliva is forming and where on your tongue you can feel it. As you take a bite from the fruit, notice how it feels resting inside of your mouth. Keep it there for a moment before you begin to chew it, noticing how it feels, and what the sensations in your mouth are like, once the fruit is resting inside of it. When you begin to chew it, pay attention to the flavors that it releases, how the texture of the fruit changes as you continue to chew it, and the way it feels between your teeth. Notice when the intention to swallow begins, and how that feels. Finally, as you begin to swallow, pay attention of the movement of the fruit into the back of your mouth, and your esophagus.

Repeat this practice as you take your next bites out of the fruit. You might even reflect, in between bites, on how this fruit was grown and cared for, both by conditions of nature and by the actions of human beings, until you were able to bring it home. This may help you to recognize how things around you are connected—even something as simple as a piece of fruit.

My observations during mindful eating: _____

_____

_____

_____

_____

Walk Mindfully

For this activity, choose a space, perhaps in your home, where you have some room to walk around—such as a long hallway or a room with enough space to walk in a circle. It will be helpful if you can have somebody read these instructions to you while you practice.

Begin by standing still, noticing the physical sensations on the bottom of your feet, where they make contact with the floor, and noticing the weight of your body that is supported by your legs and feet. When you are ready, slowly shift the weight of your body onto your right foot, noticing the sensations that you experience in your right leg and foot as you relieve your left leg from your weight. Then, as you lift your left foot from the ground, guide your attention to the sensations in your left foot and leg as they lift, and then as they descend downward and forward, and the heel makes contact with the ground.

With your left foot firmly on the ground, gently guide your awareness to the sensations you feel as you shift your body weight to the left side, noticing how the weight of your body is received by your left leg and foot, and noticing the sensation of lightness on your right leg and foot as they are relieved of the weight. Now, gently lift your right foot from the ground and, as you move it forward, pay attention to the sensations in your right leg and foot as you place your right heel to the floor, shifting your weight off of the left leg and foot and on to the right side.

Notice the patterns of changing sensations in your two legs and feet as you make this step. If your mind wanders away from this process of walking, simply notice it and gently bring your attention back to the sensations in your legs and feet. Practice walking mindfully for a few minutes.

My observations during mindful walking: _____

_____

_____

_____

_____

Breathing Mindfully

Since we are all breathing all of the time, mindful breathing can be a "go-to" skill that you can use any time, in any situation, as a way of redirecting your attention to the present moment. It can be very useful when you are first trying to learn mindfulness skills, as you can use it like this: Any time you are having difficulty guiding your attention to a particular sensation, you can always just spend a few moments focusing on your breath, and then return to the specific activity that you were doing. In addiction recovery, mindful breathing can be a very useful tool when you experience an uncomfortable emotion or craving. Once you learn how to breathe mindfully, you'll have a mindfulness technique you can use specifically for coping with cravings or urges to drink or use. Let's begin with a brief practice of breathing with awareness.

Exercise 7.3: Breathing with Awareness

Like all of the other exercises you've completed so far, remember when you try this one that it is not intended to change the way you breathe or to relax you (even though you might find that one or both of these things occur). The purpose of the exercise is simply to become aware of your breath and to observe it with openness and curiosity. You can begin by doing this exercise for about five minutes, and as you practice it more often, you can increase the time you spend on it to as long as thirty minutes, if it is comfortable to do so.

Begin by finding a comfortable place to sit. Bring your awareness to the way your body feels in the chair, and to where it makes contact with the chair and the floor. Spend a few moments exploring these sensations.

When you are ready, turn your attention to your breath. Notice how your breath enters your body through your nose and moves through your body to your lungs. You may notice that your abdomen rises and falls with each inhale and exhale. If it is helpful in connecting your attention to the experience of breathing, you can try placing your hand on your abdomen.

Observe whatever you can about your breath, with openness and curiosity. Gently guide your attention to the temperature of your breath, noticing if it becomes cooler or warmer as you breathe in and as you breathe out. Notice the air entering your body with each inhale and exiting your body with each exhale.

Whether your breathing is slow or fast, deep or shallow, just allow your body to breathe how it breathes naturally, without judging it or trying to change it in any way. As thoughts enter your mind, just notice them and allow them to be there, gently guiding your awareness back to your breath. Practice breathing with awareness in this way for a few minutes.

Putting It All Together: Using Mindfulness for Addiction Recovery

You might be wondering how mindful breathing, showering, and walking are going to help you recover successfully from your addiction. They may seem unrelated, but now that you have practiced a little bit of mindful awareness, you can apply what you've learned to help you cope with urges and temptations to use alcohol or drugs, without slipping into automatic pilot mode (which can lead you to unhealthy decisions and behaviors, like relapsing). The practice of remaining connected with your present experience can help you get through a craving without relapsing for the following reasons:

- One of the ways that you might naturally react to a craving is to try to *avoid* the discomfort that it brings. Drinking or using is one way that you might have avoided that discomfort in the past. If you can learn to accept, tolerate, and even curiously observe the sensations you experience during a craving, you can break that cycle of drinking or using to avoid those sensations.

- Your *automatic reaction* to a temptation (such as alcohol or drugs in your immediate environment) or to a specific trigger (such as an unpleasant emotion) is to drink or use. When you practice mindful awareness, rather than *reacting* to the temptation, you can learn how to thoughtfully and mindfully *respond* to it.

What's the difference between reacting and responding? you might be wondering. Reacting is something that we do automatically, without thinking. When we feel that we are standing too close to something hot, such as a fire, we *react* intuitively by moving away from it. Our intuition says, *That doesn't feel good; it can hurt you. Get away from it.* When you are addicted to something, your intuition may not lead you to a healthy decision that favors your recovery. Remember that intuition is not something that involves weighing the consequences of your behavior. If you rely on your intuition, you may *react* to temptations and difficult situations in ways that *feel* self-protective (such as drinking or using to eliminate discomfort), but are not.

When you practice being connected with your experience of temptations and uncomfortable sensations during a craving, you can begin to trace these experiences back and understand how they have led you to automatic responses such as drinking or using in the past. In the here and now, when you practice mindfulness during a craving, you can connect with what is happening and observe it *first,* and then decide, with awareness, how you would like to *choose to respond* to it. When you approach your experience this way, rather than letting your addicted brain guide you to an automatic, conditioned response to a craving or temptation (like drinking or using), you can exercise more control over your behavior, weighing its consequences before you act. In this next exercise, you will learn a mindfulness technique that you can use when you experience a craving or temptation to drink or use.

Exercise 7.4: SOBER Breathing

Now that you have some experience with mindful breathing, this technique for connecting with the present moment will probably be very easy for you to learn. It takes just a minute or two to practice, making it an ideal go-to skill when you're in a tempting, stressful, or otherwise upsetting situation. You can use the acronym *SOBER* to help you remember the steps (Bowen, Chawla, and Marlatt 2010), summarized below:

1. **S**top: When you find yourself in a tempting situation, the first thing you need to do to connect with the present moment is to stop and step out of automatic pilot mode. When you stop, you interrupt that automatic sequence of behaviors that can follow a craving or a strong emotion, and it's that very sequence that you are working on changing when you are in addiction recovery.

2. **O**bserve: Once you've stopped and stepped out of automatic pilot, the next step is to observe your experience. Observe what is happening, right in the moment. Ask yourself what you are feeling right now. Using the example of a craving, observe where you feel it in your body, any thoughts you have about drinking or using, and any emotions you might be experiencing. Notice yourself allowing the presence of these uncomfortable aspects of your experience—letting them be just as they are, rather than pushing them away.

3. **B**reathe: You've taken yourself out of automatic pilot and observed your present experience. The next step is to connect with your breath. Take a moment to do this, guiding your attention to the movement of your breath.

4. **E**xpand your awareness: Broadening your focus from the movement of your breath, you can now expand your awareness to include your entire body as a whole, connecting with all of the sensations you are experiencing in the present moment.

5. **R**espond mindfully: We've been talking about responding with mindful awareness, rather than reacting in automatic pilot. This is the final step in the SOBER breathing exercise. Now that you have connected with your experience and your breath, you can consider the range of choices that you have in this situation. Recognize that you can accept the discomfort that you're feeling. And while you are allowing it to be there, just as it is, you can still respond by choosing, with mindful awareness, what action to take. You are in a better place to consider the consequences of the different choices you can make, and choose to respond to the discomfort you are experiencing in a way that is nurturing, self-protective, and consistent with your recovery goals.

One way that you can begin to practice the SOBER breathing exercise is to imagine a situation in which you would tempted to drink or use. As you picture yourself in this situation, practice the SOBER mindful awareness technique. First, *stop*. Next, *observe* what is happening to you as you imagine yourself in this situation, focusing on any discomfort you feel physically, emotionally, or in your thoughts. The goal is to acknowledge the discomfort without judging yourself for it or trying to change it. Third, focus on your *breath*. Then *expand* your awareness to include your whole body, noticing any sensations you might be experiencing. And finally, imagining yourself in this risky situation, think about the choices that you can make, as part of the process of *responding mindfully*. Ask yourself how you can best take care of yourself and preserve your recovery in this situation.

Imagine yourself making the best choice you could in that situation, the response that will keep you clean and sober. Maybe it's leaving the situation, or calling a friend, or finding a way to distract yourself. Whatever response you decide upon, guide your attention to the way that you feel after making this choice, noticing the sensations you experience in your body, how you are feeling emotionally, and any thoughts you might be having. Following this exercise, jot down a few notes about anything you noticed as you used the SOBER breathing technique, including any sensations, thoughts, emotions, or judgments you might have had about your experience.

My observations during my SOBER breathing exercise: _____

_____

_____

_____

_____

To become comfortable enough with the SOBER breathing technique to use it any time you need a "go-to" skill to cope with an unpleasant emotion or craving, try practicing using it in a range of situations:

Start by practicing when you're feeling stressed. Write down some notes about your sensations, thoughts, and feelings, and any judgments, distractions, or other aspects of your experience. Was it helpful in this situation?

My observations from using SOBER in a stressful situation: _____

_____

_____

_____

Try the exercise when you experience an unpleasant emotion—such as sadness, anxiety, anger, or any other emotion that you tend to react to in automatic pilot mode, without thinking about it.

My observations from using SOBER in response to an unpleasant emotion:

_____

_____

_____

Try using SOBER breathing when you experience a temptation or craving to drink or use.

My observations from using SOBER in response to an urge or temptation:

_____

_____

_____

Acceptance

Throughout this chapter, whether you've realized it or not, you've been working on acceptance. Each of the mindfulness meditation exercises you've done so far has involved some instruction about letting whatever you experience be as it is, even if it is unpleasant. That is the practice of acceptance. Why is this so important in recovery, you might be wondering? It is important because acceptance is the opposite of what your addicted brain tells you to do. Learning to practice acceptance can help you conquer your addicted brain, and put your rational brain in charge.

You might recall learning, in chapter 1, about the addicted brain's tendency to get stuck in *go* mode. The *go* mode is the part of you that says, *Get rid of that craving before it feels any worse. Go. Have a drink*, or *You don't have to feel sad. Go. Smoke some weed. You'll feel so much better.* Or if you tend to use when you feel good rather than when you feel bad, your addicted brain might be saying, *Why let this good feeling end? Go. Use some cocaine.* Until now, the voice of your addicted brain has led you to use alcohol or drugs either to avoid unpleasant feelings or to prolong positive ones.

One of the biggest challenges this poses in recovery is that the more you follow your tendency to try and avoid or get rid of the unpleasant feelings and sensations that cravings bring about, the more intense they tend to get. The same goes for other uncomfortable emotions, such as sadness, grief, anxiety, or anger. When you try to run away from these feelings, they usually come back stronger. A key aspect of practicing mindfulness is learning to accept that discomfort is there, while recognizing at the same time that your actions don't have to be dictated by your natural desire to get rid of it. Here are a few things you can tell yourself to practice acceptance:

- *It's okay for me to see things just as they are right now, as opposed to the way I think they should be.*

- *Just because I accept the way that I am feeling right now, it doesn't mean that I am satisfied with the way things are, or that I have to give up on trying to make things better.*

- *Once I see things for what they are, then I can find the energy to heal and to change what is here.*

Hillary's Story

Hillary, a thirty-four-year old woman in recovery from alcohol and cocaine addiction, lost her mom six months ago. Before that time, she had been sober for nearly three months, and she helped her mother through a very difficult battle with cancer before she died. After losing her mom, Hillary relapsed and started drinking and using cocaine again. She felt like she just couldn't tolerate the sadness and the emptiness, and drinking and using was the only way that she could escape it.

About two weeks ago, Hillary realized that the alcohol and cocaine she was using were making her feel more and more depressed, so she decided to try getting sober again. In the first few weeks of her recovery, a lot of sad thoughts and feelings come rushing in about her mom, and at those moments, Hillary feels strong urges to drink and use. When she begins practicing mindfulness, Hillary becomes more comfortable with the idea of acceptance.

She starts to use the SOBER exercise during moments of sadness and grief about her mom. When she observes those feelings in her mind and body, she brings her attention to her breath. Using her breath to connect her attention to her mind and body in the present moment, she is able to feel a little bit stronger and more able to allow herself to feel the different emotions about her loss, and to say to herself, *It's okay for me to feel what I'm feeling right now. It may not be what I want to feel, but I can tolerate and accept it for what it is. I seem to be coping with it better than I thought I could. I will just keep on trying to be present with it, since trying to escape it doesn't really help.*

With these thoughts in mind, she continues to practice breathing into the experience and staying present with it, without turning to alcohol or cocaine to try to numb it. Her sadness gradually becomes something that she can tolerate and accept.

Compassion and Kindness

Kindness and compassion are both characteristics that can enable you to practice mindfulness. For those of us who have the tendency to be self-critical, even though it may come naturally to take a kind and compassionate approach to understanding and communicating with others, we don't necessarily use that same approach toward ourselves. Being mindful is about being present in a nonjudgmental way; whatever arises when practicing mindfulness, if you can have a kind and friendly spirit toward it, you will be less likely to judge or criticize yourself for it. If you're distracted or bothered by an urge or craving to drink or use when you are practicing mindfulness meditation, and are able to connect with the experience with a kind and welcoming spirit, this will have the effect of making you more open to your experience, and more able to be present with it. Judgment, and the desire to escape or avoid things that are unpleasant or unfamiliar, will be less likely to interfere with your mindfulness practice.

Compassion is a close relative of kindness, but it is not exactly the same thing. Compassion is a tender and sympathetic emotional reaction to the presence of pain or sorrow. When you practice mindfulness, having compassion for *yourself* will help to relieve you of negative and critical inner dialogues. These dialogues not only interfere with your ability to remain present, but they can easily drive you to use alcohol or drugs. When you approach your own pain and sorrow with compassion, you can make choices about how to respond mindfully to those experiences in a way that is nurturing and self-protective, preserving your recovery.

Wrap-up

In this chapter you had the opportunity to learn about what mindfulness is, and how developing a practice of mindfulness can be helpful to you in your recovery. By acquiring the skills that enable you to approach daily life mindfully, you are making great strides in accepting the discomfort that you naturally face during recovery and taking a more open, accepting approach to dealing with it. This is not an easy thing to do, but with practice, you can use this approach to stay in control of your responses to cravings and other difficult experiences, rather than reacting to these experiences impulsively, with your addicted brain in the driver's seat.

In the next chapter, you're going to find ways to increase joy, pleasure, and fulfillment in your life. With mindfulness skills in your back pocket, you will be able to experience these positive emotions at a deeper level.

CHAPTER 8

Step 6: Rediscover Rewards

By now, you have learned a lot about how to cope with triggers and cravings. You know all about the kinds of situations, places, people, and things that make you vulnerable to relapsing, and you can plan ahead for how you are going to deal with them. But there is a big gap that still needs to be addressed to make your recovery plan complete. Now that you are not going to be drinking or using, what will you do to fill the void that the absence of alcohol and drugs will leave in your life?

Let's face it: you are working your way through this book because you know that drinking or using has become destructive in your life. But knowing that doesn't mean that giving it up is easy. It doesn't mean that you don't miss the escape or the positive feelings that you used to get from alcohol or drugs. And you might find that, when you are early in the process of recovery, your mood is up and down, and you don't enjoy many things that you used to. Not everybody feels that way, but a large majority of people who are in recovery feel that way at first. So, if you're wondering what you're going to get those pleasurable feelings from, if not from drinking or using, you are not alone. In this chapter, you will discover and rediscover rewarding activities for your recovering brain and body, and learn how to overcome some of the barriers that stand in the way of experiencing joy.

The Role of Rewards in Addiction and Recovery

Rewards are a central part of all of our lives; they are the reason we are motivated to get up in the morning, take care of our responsibilities (whether those involve work, household, or other duties), and maintain a social life, family relationships, and hobbies. All of these things that we spend our time doing, we do because we anticipate that they will bring us rewards: emotional, financial, physical, and other types of rewards that provide joy and pleasure in life.

Working, for example, can bring about all kinds of rewards: There is, of course, the financial reward when you get paid for the work that you do. If colleagues or bosses at work tell you that you are doing a good job, then that brings emotional rewards, such as feelings of confidence and pride in your work, and a sense that you are liked and appreciated by others. All of those experiences will, of course, enhance your self-esteem and feelings of self-worth, which are even greater psychological rewards. Whether you have a job in an office, go to school, or carry out your primary responsibilities at home, the rewards you get from those responsibilities are at the core of your motivation to keep on fulfilling them.

What does this have to do with addiction recovery? you might ask. Think back to before you started drinking or using. What were the rewarding things in your life? Did they have to do with the pleasure you experienced from your important relationships with family, children, a partner, or friends? Were they connected to your hobbies? Your work? Now think about how your involvement in those rewarding activities changed as you started to drink or use more and more. When people become addicted to drugs or alcohol, pursuing the "natural" sources of rewards in life becomes less and less a part of the way that they spend their time. This is because of the increasing amount of time that becomes devoted to seeking drugs or alcohol, using them, and recovering from their effects (as in hangovers, crashing, depression, and the other uncomfortable withdrawal effects that come after the use).

Does this sound familiar? To relate this to your personal experience with addiction, think about the things you started to do less of as your use of alcohol or drugs increased, and write them down in the space provided.

Things I used to enjoy that I did less of as my drinking or drug use got out of control, for example: spending time with friends or family, exercising, or pursuing hobbies:

_____

_____

_____

_____

In recovery, it is not uncommon to feel like your sources of pleasure are limited without alcohol or drugs among your options. How will you spend your free time now? What can replace the role that drinking or using had in your life, and will it feel anywhere near as good? These are very normal and important questions that you might be wondering about, and it may take you some time and trial-and-error to figure out the answers. So be patient with yourself. The exercises you complete in this chapter will help you to find new ways to experience joy and pleasure in recovery.

Studies show not only that rewards relate to the *development* of addiction, but also that they're very important in determining how successful people are at making changes to their alcohol or drug use once they enter recovery. According to what is known as *behavioral economics theory*, when people in addiction recovery have access to a range of sources of pleasure, joy, and satisfaction, they are more likely to quit drinking or using drugs successfully (Green and Kagel 1996; Higgins, Alessi, and Dantona 2002). This theory has a lot of scientific evidence behind it. For example, in one study that compared two different types of behavioral treatments for addiction, the people with the most success in staying sober were those who got involved in a range of pleasurable activities and did them frequently. It didn't matter what type of treatment they received—the single most important thing that determined whether people were able to stay sober was their consistent involvement in a wide range of enjoyable activities. These activities replaced the time and energy they had been spending on addictive behaviors, enabling them to experience pleasure without having to face the devastating consequences of alcohol or drug use (Farabee, Rawson, and McCann 2002).

Behavioral Activation in Addiction Recovery

As studies have continued to prove how important it is for addicts in recovery to find healthy ways of experiencing joy and fulfillment, a treatment approach that has been used to help people with depression to do this very thing has recently been applied to the treatment of addiction as well. This approach, called behavioral activation therapy, is focused on motivating people to get involved in pleasant activities on a regular basis (Daughters et al. 2008; Magidson et al. 2011).

Behavioral activation therapy has been found to be very helpful to people who struggle with depression, because depression can cause a loss of motivation to do enjoyable things (Cuijpers, Smit, and van Straten 2007; Mazzucchelli, Kane, and Rees 2009; Sturmey 2009). This becomes part of a vicious cycle: when people stop doing pleasurable things, their mood tends to get worse, which makes them more vulnerable to addictive behaviors; and as addictive behaviors take over, less and less time is devoted to doing enjoyable activities. Recent studies have shown that, when used to help people who struggle with both addiction and depression, Behavioral activation therapy helps them successfully quit their use of drugs and alcohol *and* improves symptoms of depression at the same time (Daughters et al. 2008; Magidson et al. 2011).

Bringing Pleasure into Recovery

As you begin to think about how you'd like to incorporate pleasant activities into your life, keep the following suggestions in mind. You'll get to explore these suggestions in more depth when you complete the exercises in this chapter:

- Be sure that you select activities carefully, so as not to choose something that may trigger a craving or a temptation.

- An important goal is to create a balance between things that you *enjoy* doing and things that you do to fulfill responsibilities. There is an important difference between the two.

- To increase your chances of actually getting around to doing pleasant activities, try scheduling them.

- When you schedule pleasant activities, consider what your most risky times of day are (in other words, when you are the most vulnerable to relapsing), and try to plan them during those times.

- Keep in mind that your assumptions about whether you'll enjoy a particular activity may be wrong. In exercise 8.5 (Pleasure Predicting), you can explore this idea further and see how it applies to you.

Pleasant Activities vs. Risky Situations

Now that you are getting used to living a lifestyle that supports your recovery, you are going to learn to be thoughtful in new and different ways about the activities you choose to do. As you start to plan how you will spend your time, you might try asking yourself, before you decide to do something (such as going to a movie or a concert, or hanging out with certain friends): *Is this something that might trigger me to want to drink or use?* Sometimes, without realizing it, we can be drawn to certain activities that used to be associated with drinking or using. Let's consider an example:

Daniel Gets Triggered

Daniel has been abstinent from using marijuana for five weeks now. His friend Holden calls him up and invites him to go to a concert featuring an artist Daniel has seen several times before and would love to see again. *This is great,* Daniel thinks to himself. *I didn't know what I was going to do tonight, and now I have something to occupy my time.* What Daniel doesn't realize is that both Holden and this concert are risky for his recovery. He used to smoke pot with Holden all the time, and he has never been to see this particular artist in concert when he wasn't high. When he gets to the concert, he finds himself with a craving he rates as an 8 in intensity on a scale from 1 to 10. Holden has some weed, so Daniel ends up smoking with him that night.

In this situation, Daniel was trying to find something pleasurable to do, but he didn't make the link between the music he was going to listen to at the concert and his prior marijuana use. He also didn't recognize how the cards were stacked against him with his friend Holden coming with him. While Daniel had quit five weeks ago and no longer had his own supply, Holden made it easy for him to access the marijuana.

Now, with the knowledge that he chose a risky situation when he intended to plan a pleasant activity, Daniel can think through how he might have planned to do things differently if he had asked himself the question, *Could this concert trigger me to want to use?* beforehand. If he had realized that Holden and the music itself could be triggers, there are a few ways he could have handled the situation differently:

- He could have avoided the concert completely. This would be the safest choice, especially in early recovery. At this stage, Daniel's ability to resist temptations is likely at its weakest, and he hasn't yet learned all of the coping strategies that he needs to have in place to take on something so risky.

- He could have gone to the concert, but not with Holden. One way of protecting himself from a potential relapse would be to find a supportive sober friend to go with him, and discuss a plan with that friend for how he would handle himself if he were to have a craving (for example, leave early, or tell the friend about it and talk it through).

Daniel's example is included to give you a good sense of how to ask yourself the right questions about a planned activity so that you can learn to tell the difference between a healthy, pleasant activity and a risky situation. If you schedule your time in advance, and give thoughtful consideration to what you are planning, you can avoid placing yourself in a triggering situation.

Exercise 8.1: Activity Tracking

The first step in developing a healthy, rewarding life is to get an accurate sense of how you are spending your time, and how your current activities relate to your mood and use of alcohol or drugs. To do this, using the form below, you are going to record all of your daily activities, including the ones that may seem unimportant (like watching TV). You don't need to change the way you are doing anything just yet; you will brainstorm about how to make positive changes a little bit later in this chapter. For now, the tracking will help you to get a sense of your current patterns of activities, moods, and behaviors.

Using the activity tracking form works best when you fill out the form twice per day—once in the afternoon, and once in the evening. When you use this form, you will rate how much you enjoyed each activity, from 0 to 10, with 0 meaning it was not at all enjoyable and 10 meaning it was extremely enjoyable. There is no "correct" rating for any activity; you are simply doing this to notice patterns. So, for example, if you spent the hour from 6:00 to 7:00 cooking dinner, and you really did not enjoy it, you would rate it a 0 or a 1.

A "pleasant" or "enjoyable" activity is anything that you rate a 6 or higher. At the end of the day, you will add up how many pleasant activities (rated 6 or higher) you did, and you will rate your overall mood on that day on a scale from 0 to 10, with 0 meaning your mood was as low as it can get, and 10 meaning that your mood couldn't have been better. You'll also rate your most intense craving of the day from 1 to 10, with 1 meaning it was very mild and 10 meaning that it was extremely strong. Finally, you'll indicate whether or not you drank or used on that day. Complete this form on a daily basis for at least one week. You can download fresh copies of it at http://www.newharbinger.com/32783.

Activity Tracking Form

Day/Date: _____

Time	Activity	Pleasure Rating (0–10)
7:00–8:00 a.m.		
8:00–9:00 a.m.		
9:00–10:00 a.m.		
10:00–11:00 a.m.		
11:00–12:00 p.m.		
12:00–1:00 p.m.		
1:00–2:00 p.m.		
2:00–3:00 p.m.		

3:00–4:00 p.m.		
4:00–5:00 p.m.		
5:00–6:00 p.m.		
6:00–7:00 p.m.		
7:00–8:00 p.m.		
8:00–9:00 p.m.		
9:00–10:00 p.m.		

Total pleasant activities (rated 6 or higher): _____

Overall mood rating for today (0 to 10): _____

Peak craving rating for today (1 to 10): _____

Relapse: Yes   No

The more frequently you track your activities, the better able you will be to recognize patterns that you might want to change. Using the previous form, you will start to see the connections between your moods and your activity level, both of which are related to your use of alcohol and drugs. People who do more pleasurable things tend to be happier, and the happiness makes them want to do more enjoyable things.

If you have a therapist or counselor, review your activity tracking form with him or her, and try to set some goals around the changes you'd like to make to it. If you don't have a therapist or counselor, try to look for patterns: When you do more pleasant activities, are your mood ratings any different? What about your cravings? Maybe the activities help both, or maybe only one. Either way, understanding how your activities relate to your mood and cravings is part of strengthening your skill set as a self expert. You can then make adjustments to your activities according to what your needs are on any given day.

Balancing "Should Dos" with "Want Tos"

As you are reading this chapter, you might find yourself thinking, *I'm a pretty active person. I do a lot of stuff. Do I really need to do more?* The answer to that depends. Are the things you are spending your time doing things that you are *obligated* to do, or are they things that you find *enjoyable*? The key is to have a balance between the two. Often the scale is tipped in the direction of lots of "should dos," or activities that are part of your responsibilities. This can feel very unfulfilling, and can lead to guilt, confusion, or dissatisfaction with life. On the other hand, when people are doing a lot of pleasurable activities and not working on any long-term goals, this can create a void, or a feeling of underachieving or not accomplishing enough. Let's take a look at your personal balance of responsibility and fun, so that you can decide where you need to focus your efforts.

Exercise 8.2: "Should Dos" and "Want Tos"

For this exercise, you are simply going to make a list of the things that you do to fulfill responsibilities (your "should dos") and the things that you do for fun ("want tos"), so that you can get a sense of how balanced they are.

Should Dos

1._____

2._____

3._____

4._____

5._____

6._____

7._____

8._____

9._____

10._____

Want Tos

1. _____

2. _____

3. _____

4. _____

5. _____

6. _____

7. _____

8. _____

9. _____

10. _____

What did you notice during this exercise? Was it hard for you to come up with things that you do for pleasure, or was it the other way around? Pay attention to where you see a gap in your activity balance, so that you can begin to brainstorm about ways to have satisfying numbers and types of activities in both categories.

Exercise 8.3: Pleasant Activities

Ideally, you should have one pleasant activity worked into each day. It doesn't have to take up a lot of time; it just needs to be something you do with the intention of enjoying yourself. In this next exercise, take a look at the list of pleasant activities and see if there is anything that you'd like to start or continue doing. Circle each one.

Go for a walk.	Cook something new.	Read something enjoyable.
Go to a museum.	Go to the zoo.	Take a dance class.
Go to the movies.	Spend time with a friend.	Go on a date.
Plan a trip somewhere.	Plan a party.	Go for a bike ride.
Go to the library.	Exercise.	Call someone you like.
Invite people over for dinner.	Eat out at a restaurant.	Do some gardening.
Draw something.	Plan and do an art project.	Listen to some music.
Play a sport you like.	Go to a sports event.	Watch something on TV.
Eat dessert.	Go hiking.	Make a bouquet of flowers.
Decorate part of your home.	Write a story.	Go to the theater.
Get a new haircut or hairdo.	Take a bath.	Go to a religious activity.
Sing a song.	Go to a park.	Play a musical instrument.
Meditate.	Spend time with family.	Get a massage.
Organize your photos.	Surf the Internet.	Skype with someone.
Have takeout and movie night.	Go to the beach.	Write a poem.
Do some journaling.	Make a gift for someone.	Go to an aquarium.
Go skating.	Do a puzzle.	Make jewelry.
Go to the mall.	Take a class.	Play with a pet.
Go bowling.	Do some volunteer work.	Take some photographs.

Activities not listed in the Pleasant Events table that I would like to do:

1. _____

2. _____

3. _____

4. _____

5. _____

6. _____

Exercise 8.4: Activity Scheduling

Now that you have identified some new activities you'd like to do, the next step is to plan when to do them. Then, be sure to continue tracking your activities throughout the day, so that you can keep tabs on how you're balancing Should Dos and Want Tos.

Activity I plan to do: **Date I plan to do it, or start it:**

Activity #1 (_____)   Date:_____

Activity #2 (_____)   Date:_____

Activity #3 (_____)   Date:_____

Activity #4 (_____)   Date:_____

Activity #5 (_____)   Date:_____

Activity #6 (_____)   Date:_____

Activity #7 (_____)   Date:_____

Activity #8 (_____)   Date:_____

Activity #9 (_____)   Date:_____

Activity #10 (_____)   Date:_____

When Things Get in the Way

Sometimes, things just get in the way of our doing things for fun. It could be a practical problem, like figuring out who will watch the kids or walk the dog, or how to free up your busy schedule. For this reason, scheduling activities in advance can be helpful, because it will lead you to plan for these kinds of obstacles. Looking at the list of pleasant activities that you planned in the previous exercise, take a few moments to think about potential barriers, or things that might prevent you from doing one or more of them despite your best intentions. Make a list of these obstacles below.

OBSTACLES TO PLEASANT ACTIVITIES:

1. _____

2. _____

3. _____

4. _____

Now, for each of the obstacles that you listed, there is a three-step process you can follow to find a realistic solution:

- **First:** brainstorm a list of all of the possible solutions that you can think of.

- **Second:** think about the pros and cons of each of the solutions, and narrow it down to the best one or two approaches.

- **Third:** try one of the best approaches, and see how well it works to free you up or otherwise enable you to do the pleasant activity.

Let's practice this now, with the first barrier that you identified.

Barrier #1: _____

Step 1: Here are all of the possible solutions I can think of for this problem:

1. _____

2. _____

3. _____

4. _____

5. _____

Step 2: These are the pros and cons of each of the possible solutions:

Solution #	Pros	Cons
1		
2		
3		
4		
5		

Step 3: Pick the best two solutions:

1. _____

2. _____

Once you've tried one or both of these, evaluate how well they worked, so that you can decide which solution you'd like to use again in the future.

In addition to practical obstacles, our thoughts can sometimes run interference with doing pleasant activities. Often we think that we won't enjoy something because we are too tired, or we're not in a good mood, or we just don't feel like doing anything. But sometimes we are wrong. Remember how we worked on recognizing cognitive distortions in chapter 5? We are going to revisit cognitive distortions, specifically as they relate to pleasant activities, here.

Negative moods can affect our expectations about how much we can enjoy things. That is, if your mood isn't great, you probably don't expect that going out for dinner or being with other people is going to be enjoyable, simply because you don't feel like it. But the reality can be quite different from what you expected, because the activity itself can change your mood. Below are a few examples of thoughts that can get in the way of getting out and doing something fun:

- *I don't feel like it.*

- *It won't be any fun.*

- *I'm just going to want to leave and go home.*

- *It will be a waste of time.*

- *I'm going to ruin everyone else's fun with my bad mood.*

Do any of these thoughts sound familiar? If not, then perhaps negative thoughts are not such a big barrier for you personally. If they are familiar, you should know that these are very common ways of thinking, and there is a way that you can change these thoughts, just as you've learned to change some of your irrational ways of thinking about drinking or using. Below you will be introduced to a technique that will help you learn how to challenge your thoughts about pleasant activities.

Exercise 8.5: Pleasure Predicting

As you are learning, our thoughts and feelings about activities can be very misleading at times. The idea behind *pleasure predicting* is that we can act like scientists, examining our negative thoughts and expectations about activities and gathering evidence to see whether or not they turn out to be accurate. According to this approach, just because you don't feel like doing something doesn't mean that it isn't worth doing. You can *choose* to do something and then decide whether it was enjoyable, based on your observations about your thoughts and your mood during and after the activity. Here's how to do it:

- First, when you're planning to do an activity, before you do it, write down how much you expect to enjoy it, using a percentage from 0 to 100, with 0 meaning that you don't expect to enjoy it all, 50 percent meaning that you think you will enjoy it moderately, and 100 percent meaning that you expect that you will enjoy it to the fullest extent possible. Pay attention to any other thoughts you are having about the activity and write them down.

- Then, *do the activity,* even if you rated it a 0. Without this step, you can't do pleasure predicting!

- During the activity, pay attention to any thoughts you are having about it and jot them down.

- After you finish the activity, rate how much you *actually enjoyed it,* from 0 to 100 percent.

- Compare the enjoyment ratings from before and after you did the activity. These pleasure ratings might be different, or they might not be; either way, it's okay. The idea is to be an objective observer of your experience and begin to identify patterns.

Exercise 8.6: Pleasure Predicting Form

Pleasant Activity	Pleasure Prediction Rating Before (0 to 100%)	Pleasure Rating After (0 to 100%)	Thoughts Before and During the Activity

What did you notice about your ratings before and after the activities? In some cases, you might find that while you approach certain activities with a sense of dread, or with low expectations about how much fun you will have, you get more enjoyment out of them than you expect. These are, of course, the types of activities that you'll want to repeat, and you can remind yourself of how your predictions might have been more about your mood than about the activity itself. In other situations, you might find that the activity was just as you expected it to be.

Remember that in recovery, you are going to be redefining the way that you spend your time, and an important part of this will involve figuring out what kinds of things you can enjoy without feeling triggered to drink or use. The things you enjoy that are not risky for you now may not be the same things that were pleasurable and safe for you when you were actively drinking or using. If you look at pleasure predicting as a process of discovery, you can find ways to experience joy and fun in recovery, which will help you stay healthy and sober.

Exercise 8.7: Reward Yourself for Scheduling and Following Through

Now that you have some experience with pleasure predicting, you might have some activities in mind that you'd like to repeat, because you found that you enjoyed them. Scheduling activities helps to make it more likely that you'll follow through, because you've already committed to it and worked your way through any barriers in terms of scheduling. To take it a step further, after you do an activity that you planned and committed to, you should reward yourself for following through, just as you did in chapter 4 when you worked on incorporating physical exercise into your routine. In this exercise, you will schedule your next few activities for the coming week, and plan how you will reward yourself afterward.

Week: _____

This week, I will do the following activities:

1. I will _____ (activity) on _____ (date),

and I will reward myself by _____.

2. I will _____ (activity) on _____ (date),

and I will reward myself by _____.

3. I will _____ (activity) on _____ (date),

and I will reward myself by _____.

Wrap-up

In this chapter you learned about how you can reintroduce pleasurable activities into your life in a way that is compatible with your recovery. Finding balance between work and fun is a lifelong practice. Things aren't always in perfect balance; there will be times when you find yourself doing more work and fulfilling responsibilities, with less time for fun, and other times when you have a little more free time on your hands. With continued awareness of your goal to keep things in balance as much as possible, you will get better and better at it, and this will serve your recovery well. The more joy and pleasure you come to derive from relationships, hobbies, and other activities, the less you will miss the presence of alcohol or drugs in your life.

CHAPTER 9

Step 7: Conquer Challenging Emotions

Now that you have some helpful strategies for coping with cravings, you will need skills on board for dealing with some of the other unpleasant feelings that are common in recovery, such as anxiety, sadness, and anger. Most of the CBT, mindfulness, and motivational techniques you've already learned can actually help you with these types of emotions. To mobilize these "go-to" skills in a different way, we will review how you can use them when negative feelings come up.

You will face your share of ups and downs in this new phase of your life. Getting equipped to anticipate and cope with them without relapsing will be the focus of this chapter.

Managing Your Mood

More often than not, addictions go hand in hand with other psychological problems. Studies show that as many as two-thirds of people with addictions have mental health issues, the most common of which are anxiety and mood disorders, such as depression (Glasner-Edwards et al. 2009). This is not surprising, right? It makes sense that alcohol or other substances could become a sort of "refuge" for dealing with unpleasant emotions or symptoms.

By now, if you are someone who used to self-medicate your depression or anxiety by drinking or using, you've probably learned that in the long run, alcohol and drugs are not the most effective antidepressants. In fact, they make depression and anxiety worse over time. But at the time when you started using them that way, they probably made pretty good Band-Aids. To avoid falling back into the trap of drinking or using as a Band-Aid for negative emotions, you can use the following techniques, which you've already practiced for coping with cravings: (1) monitoring and challenging negative thoughts that lead to triggering emotions, (2) revisiting your motivation to remain abstinent, (3) engaging in pleasant activities and other behavioral coping strategies, and (4) using mindfulness-based coping skills. We will briefly review how to apply each of these approaches to coping with negative moods below.

Know Your Negative Emotional Triggers

Back in chapter 5, you completed an exercise on identifying your internal triggers. Those emotional triggers may have included depression, anxiety, anger, jealousy, irritability, boredom, rejection, frustration, guilt or shame, or feeling overwhelmed. Turn back to that exercise (5.1) and review your internal emotional triggers. If you can be one step ahead of these triggers—meaning that you are able to recognize when the emotions are coming on, before they're full-blown and driving you into relapse mode—then you can stay ahead in your recovery, preventing a relapse before the triggering events can lead you there.

Mood Monitoring

We all feel down sometimes. In early recovery in particular, it is very common to feel sad or depressed on and off for a period of time. This can often be explained by the withdrawal syndrome—in other words, the effects of alcohol or drugs leaving your body. After a month or longer of abstinence from drug or alcohol use, these symptoms may resolve themselves. In some people, however, those depressed feelings persist for longer, and may require additional treatment using medications or therapy.

If you find that you have lingering depression symptoms, it is important to get them evaluated and properly treated, as they can lower your chances of success in addiction recovery if they are not managed (Glasner-Edwards et al. 2009). A list of common symptoms of depression follows; if a few of these persist for longer than a month after you've gotten sober, you should consult a professional for evaluation and possible treatment recommendations.

DEPRESSION SYMPTOMS

- Sadness

- Feeling unable to enjoy things that used to bring you pleasure

- Crying spells

- Low energy

- Feeling restless

- Sleep problems (either inability to sleep or sleeping more than usual)

- Changes in appetite (either increase or decrease)

- Loss of energy

- Problems with concentration

- Difficulty making everyday decisions (like what to wear or what to eat)

- Feelings of worthlessness

- Feelings of hopelessness

- Thoughts about death or dying, or suicidal thoughts

Cognitive Distortions That Lead to Depression and Anxiety

In chapter 6, you took an in-depth look at cognitive distortions that lead to red flag thoughts. As it turns out, these same categories of distortions can lead you to think in ways that fuel sadness and anxiety. Below, you'll find examples of anxious and depressing thoughts in each of the categories of irrational thoughts that you learned about in chapter 6.

- **Black-or-white thinking:** When you think of things this way, you see things as all good or all bad. For example: *My date canceled for Saturday night. I'm always going to be alone.*

- **Discounting the positive:** When you ignore or devalue the positive aspects of a situation, you end up paying attention only to the potential negatives. For example: *My friend probably only complimented my outfit because she feels sorry for me. I know I look awful.*

- **Jumping to conclusions:** Just as it sounds, this distortion happens when you make assumptions about a person or situation without any evidence to support them. One type of distorted thought in this category is *fortune telling*, or making assumptions about what will happen in the future. For example: *I'm not going to get that job. It won't work out for me, just like everything else I try.*

- **Taking your feelings too seriously:** This mistake in thinking happens when you take a feeling you're having in the moment and assume that it is a true reflection of your reality. For example: *I don't feel like I can enjoy anything. I'm just going to live my life in misery.*

- **Self-blame:** This cognitive distortion occurs when you assume an excessive amount of blame for your problems. For example: *I created my own problems by making so many bad decisions about drinking and using. My depression is my own fault.*

- **Labeling:** When you use a negative label to describe yourself, it fuels negative moods. For example: *Only losers like me need treatment for an addiction. I was too weak to keep it under control.*

Although there are other types of cognitive distortions, these examples should give you a sense of the types of thoughts linked with depression and anxiety that fit into the various categories of mistakes in thinking. In this next exercise, you are going to begin tracking your own emotionally triggering thoughts, and monitoring how they relate to your cravings for alcohol or drugs.

Exercise 9.1: Mood and Craving Log

To begin to understand what types of thoughts may trigger you to feel sad or depressed, complete the following log, including the specific thoughts, along with a depression rating from 1 to 10—with 1 meaning very slightly depressed, and 10 being the most depressed. Also complete a craving rating from 0 to 10, representing your overall level of cravings for alcohol or drugs on that same day.

Date	Situation	Thought	Depression Rating (0–10)	Craving Rating (0–10)

Now that you've had some experience with rating your moods and cravings, can you see a connection between them? Do you tend to have stronger cravings on days when you have more frequent depressing thoughts? Or is it when you have a higher depression rating (when the thoughts affect your mood more negatively)? Are there themes or situations that are coming up repeatedly that trigger depressing thoughts? Just take notice of these patterns as a way of deepening your self-understanding. Continue to complete these ratings for at least a few weeks using this form, which is available at http://www.newharbinger.com/32783. Knowing what makes you depressed and how this relates to urges to drink or use will help you to anticipate urges on a down day and put some of your new coping skills to use to get you through it without relapsing.

Anxiety Monitoring

As you are learning more about the mood symptoms that may make you vulnerable to relapse, it might help you to know that mood and anxiety symptoms often go hand in hand. That is, most people who suffer from depression also experience some level of anxiety. There are different types of anxiety disorders; the most common types that overlap with addiction are reviewed briefly below:

- **Generalized anxiety disorder:** People with this problem are chronic worriers. If you have generalized anxiety disorder, you worry about a lot of things, down to everyday decisions, and you have a hard time turning the worry off. Along with your worried thoughts, you experience anxiety symptoms such as fatigue, tension, irritability, or nausea. Other symptoms may also be present.

- **Social anxiety disorder:** If you have social anxiety, it means that you get very nervous when you are going to be around other people (whether socializing, meeting new people, or speaking in front of others at work or in another setting). This form of anxiety often stems from feeling self-conscious about how others will view or judge you. Your self-consciousness is so anxiety provoking that it leads to very uncomfortable symptoms, like shortness of breath, sweating, heart palpitations, nausea, dizziness, or other symptoms.

- **Panic attacks or panic disorder:** Panic attacks involve a sudden rush of intense fear that occurs completely out of the blue, along with anxiety symptoms including shortness of breath; sweating; feeling faint; heart racing; nausea; or fear of losing control, going crazy, or dying. When you have repeated panic attacks and begin to fear them, you can develop panic disorder.

- **Post-traumatic stress disorder:** This anxiety disorder can develop in someone who has been exposed to a traumatic event. This event could involve witnessing or experiencing a life-threatening situation or a natural disaster, and in that situation feeling very helpless or horrified. In some people, these experiences lead to anxiety symptoms that may include feeling numb, having nightmares or flashbacks, feeling depressed or hopeless about the future, having trouble connecting emotionally with others, or avoiding things that remind them of the traumatic event.

If you think that you may suffer from any of these problems, it is advisable for you to get evaluated by a mental health professional to confirm a diagnosis and consider some treatment recommendations. You may find, though, that you have some symptoms of worry, anxiety, or panic even if it is not a diagnosable disorder. These symptoms could worsen temporarily in early recovery, as alcohol or drugs leave your body and you begin to experience some of the emotions that you might have been suppressing while you were drinking or using. With the log below, you can start recording your anxious thoughts, just as you did for your depression, to get a sense of how frequently they are happening, what situations they are linked to, and how they might relate to your cravings or urges to use.

Exercise 9.2: Anxiety and Craving Log

To begin to understand what types of thoughts may trigger you to feel anxious, complete the following log, including thoughts that make you feel anxious or nervous, along with an anxiety rating from 1 to 10, with 1 meaning very slightly anxious, and 10 being the most anxious you've felt. Also complete a craving rating from 0 to 10, representing your overall level of cravings for alcohol or drugs on that same day.

Date	Situation	Thought	Anxiety Rating (0–10)	Craving Rating (0–10)

Just as you did with your log of depressing thoughts, take a look at your responses here and look for patterns. How do your anxious thoughts relate to your cravings for alcohol or drugs? Do you notice any themes or situations that are common to many of your anxious thoughts? Use this exercise to continue to build your self expertise. Do you need to read up more on anxiety and how to manage it? Or are depressing thoughts more of an issue for you? Understanding the emotions that you experience that make you the most vulnerable will empower you in your healing process. If you are currently in counseling or therapy, you can review these exercises with your counselor or therapist.

Challenging Negative Thoughts

Earlier in this workbook, you learned to challenge red flag thoughts using the three T's: (1) identifying the triggering situation, (2) describing the thought, and (3) placing the thought on trial. You can use the same strategy to challenge negative, depressing, or anxious thinking—what we'll call dysfunctional thoughts. Let's consider Alicia's example:

Alicia's Negative Thinking

Alicia has been sober from alcohol for nearly a month. She is invited to a work party at a restaurant with a bar, where she knows that many of her colleagues will be drinking and dancing. Alicia decides to invite Vince, a new love interest of hers who is also sober. She and Vince have been out for coffee together a few times, on his invitation, but this is the first time Alicia has asked him out. He enthusiastically accepts her invitation, but then, on the day before the party, he tells her that he got called in to work on a project and he won't be able to make it. He apologizes and asks her if she'd like to go out for dinner another night, after his project is completed. Alicia feels very hurt and rejected. She thinks, *I was probably completely wrong about him. I have nothing going for me. I'm sure Vince only said yes in the first place because he feels sorry for me. I'm always going to be alone.*

In the past, Alicia would have wound up going to the party and drinking as a result of these types of depressive and anxious thoughts, but this time she tries thought challenging, using the three T's:

Triggering situation: feeling rejected when Vince cancelled plans to go to the party with her

Dysfunctional thoughts: *I have nothing going for me, I'm sure Vince only said yes in the first place because he feels sorry for me. I'm always going to be alone.*

Thoughts on trial: Alicia *examines the evidence* that Vince didn't really want to go with her to the party:

Questions to Ask to Examine the Evidence	The Facts
What evidence is there that Vince only said yes because he felt sorry for me?	*None, really. He said yes pretty enthusiastically.*
Is there any evidence that Vince actually likes me and wanted to go with me?	*Yes. First of all, we've been out before, and Vince was the one who initiated those coffee dates every time we've been out so far. Second, when he canceled, he actually followed up immediately with an alternative plan, to go out to dinner with me.*
Is it true that I have nothing going for me?	*Well, I'd like to have more going for me, but right now there are a few very good things I have going: I'm sober, I have a job, and I'm very connected with my family.*
Is there evidence that I'm always going to be alone?	*I am fortune telling. I don't really know if I am going to be alone or not. I have had several relationships, and even though they haven't worked out, I haven't been alone for most of my life. Also, whether or not I am in a romantic relationship, I am not truly alone. I do have family and friends, although I really would like to have a romantic partner in my future.*

Now that Alicia has considered her thoughts using the three T's, she can see that she made a few mistakes in thinking: she was *discounting the positive* when she told herself that Vince was just feeling sorry for her; she was using *black-or-white thinking* when she told herself that she had nothing going for herself, and she was *jumping to conclusions* when she thought that she would always be alone. In the right hand column, titled "The Facts," Alicia successfully challenged and replaced her negative thoughts with more rational thinking.

In this next exercise, you can practice challenging some of your own depressed or anxious thoughts using the three T's.

Exercise 9.3: Challenging Your Negative Thoughts

In this exercise, you are going to think about two recent situations in which you felt depressed or anxious, and describe them. For each situation, you will write down the negative thought that went through your mind, along with the emotion that you felt. After you identify the thought error you made, you will practice the three T's of thought challenging. You can refer back to Exercise 6.1 to refresh your memory about how you did this when you were working on your red flag thoughts.

Situation #1: _____

Negative thoughts and emotions that the thoughts led to:

_____

Thoughts on trial: _____

_____

Evidence that the thoughts are accurate: _____

_____

_____

Evidence that the thoughts are not accurate: _____

_____

_____

Response (What can you tell yourself to see the situation more realistically?):

_____

_____

_____

Situation #2: _____

Negative thoughts and emotions that the thoughts led to:

_____

Thoughts on trial: _____

_____

Evidence that the thoughts are accurate: _____

_____

_____

Evidence that the thoughts are not accurate: _____

_____

_____

Response (What can you tell yourself to see the situation more realistically?):

_____

_____

_____

Managing Anger

Do you ever find yourself losing your cool when you're angry? Most of us do, at one time or another. If this is a frequent experience for you, and if anger is one of your relapse triggers, then having some healthy coping tools and outlets for it is going to come in really handy for you as you work toward your recovery.

One of the most important things to keep in mind is that there are many disadvantages to losing your temper, aside from how it feels and the potential for relapse that it brings. When you raise your voice or otherwise act out aggressively in anger:

- You appear out of control.

- People don't respect or take seriously what you are saying.

- You don't get your needs met.

- You lose self-respect.

The first step to getting a handle on your anger is to understand how it feels, so that you can anticipate when it's coming on. Take a moment and think about how you experience anger. Where do you feel it in your body? What kinds of thoughts go through your head when you are feeling angry? Jot down some notes about it below.

When I am angry:

These are the physical sensations I experience: _____

_____

_____

_____

These are some of the thoughts that frequently go through my mind:

_____

_____

_____

_____

These are some of the ways that I express it when I can't control it:

_____

_____

_____

_____

The next step to learning how to effectively manage anger is to figure out what triggers it. In the exercise that follows, you are going to identify your anger triggers. First, let's look at an example of how uncontrollable anger can unfold and create unwanted consequences.

Jenny Gets Angry

Jenny has been sober from alcohol for six weeks. She and her husband have been in some conflict recently about the division of responsibilities between them. On Saturday, their son Sammy has basketball practice at two o'clock. Jenny wants to get together with some friends around one o'clock and she tells her husband that he needs to take Sammy to practice. He refuses, saying that he has things to do. He leaves the house before she can get a word in edgewise. Jenny is enraged. Thoughts are racing through her head. *He has no respect for me, or my time! If he keeps this up I will never have a life. I'm going to let him have it!* Unable to reach him, she leaves him a very angry, screaming voice mail. Her son, after witnessing all of this, says, "Mommy, why are you so mad at Dad? You don't like going with me to basketball?" Jenny feels very guilty and ashamed of her behavior. Suddenly she finds herself experiencing a very strong craving for alcohol.

Thinking about Jenny's situation, you can probably see the various consequences of her inability to control her anger. She felt out of control; she reacted toward her husband in a way that probably did not resolve anything; and in the process, she unintentionally hurt her son's feelings and modeled poor anger control. She ended up feeling ashamed, and this affected her recovery by setting her up for a strong alcohol craving.

Exercise 9.4: Anger Triggers

Identifying your personal anger triggers is the first step toward learning how to cope with anger more effectively. Usually, anger triggers fall into one of five categories:

- People (such as Jenny's husband)

- Places (such as the car, if you're someone who experiences frustration and anger management problems on the road)

- Feelings (such as feeling rejected, ignored, restless, or impatient)

- Thoughts (such as thoughts about the inefficiency of other people—for example, *Why is this line taking so long? I have somewhere to be!*)

- Physical *sensations* (such as physical discomfort from alcohol or drug withdrawal, which can create irritability and anger)

Write down your anger triggers in each of these categories below:

People:

_____

_____

_____

_____

Places:

_____

_____

_____

_____

Thoughts:

_____

_____

_____

_____

Feelings:

_____

_____

_____

_____

Physical sensations:

_____

_____

_____

_____

Give It a Beat

Now that you are aware of your personal anger triggers, you need to learn to give it a beat—to take a few moments to calm down when you feel angry and think about next steps. You don't need to react on impulse or "take the bait" from someone who says or does something that provokes you to feel angry. Instead, you can choose to remain in control, rise above it, and cope with it in such a way that you will be able to look back and think, *I'm proud of the way I handled that.* This doesn't mean that you shouldn't *feel* angry. Anger control is not about preventing the experience of anger; it is about controlling your *response* to it. Here are some coping strategies that you can try when you *give it a beat:*

- **Have an inner dialogue about it before you decide how to respond.** Try telling yourself one of the following phrases—whichever is the most helpful to you:

  - *I can keep my cool and remain in control of myself.*

  - *It's up to me to remain in control. I know I can do it.*

  - *I can stay relaxed and get through this in a way that I can feel good about in the end.*

  - *I can't control how other people act and feel. Even if the actions of others upset me, I can only control my own behavior.*

- **Be assertive.** Tell the other person that you're feeling upset and you need some time to gather your thoughts and feelings before you can talk about it.

- **Leave the situation.** Just as you may have to leave a triggering situation in which you are vulnerable to relapse, if your anger is triggered and you're concerned that you might not be able to control it, leaving the situation is a perfectly reasonable coping strategy.

- **Focus on your breath.** Relaxation and meditation strategies can be very helpful to bring your nervous system back into rhythm when you are feeling worked up.

- **Count to ten.** This can buy you the time that you need to calm yourself down so you don't react in an out-of-control or impulsive manner.

- **Allow yourself to cry.** If you need an emotional outlet, give yourself the space and permission to do that. Crying is much healthier than lashing out in anger at someone else.

When you've calmed yourself down in the moment, *then* you can begin to think about how you can challenge angry thoughts. Use the *assertive communication* skills that you practiced in chapter 4 to communicate about the situation that made you angry in an effective manner that enables you to get your needs met.

Coming back to Jenny's situation, let's take a look at how she might challenge her angry thoughts by considering the consequences of her behavior and coming up with an inner dialogue that can help to lessen her angry feelings:

Triggering situation: Feeling that her needs were ignored by her husband. He refused to take Sammy to basketball practice, which made her unable to carry out her social plans.

Angry thoughts: *He has no respect for me, or my time! If he keeps this up I will never have a life. I'm going to let him have it!*

Alternative responses:

- *It's understandable that I'm angry; he knows that disregarding my requests like that gets me worked up. But I won't let myself hang on to anger because of him.*

- *I'll discuss a way to plan our weekends in advance when he comes home and I've cooled down.*

- *I'm going to make the best of the afternoon and take Sammy for ice cream after basketball practice.*

- *I'm going to apologize to Sammy for losing my cool like that and try to talk with him about healthier ways to express anger, so I can still set a good example.*

- *I know that it's okay to feel anger, but I'm going to do a mindfulness breathing meditation for five or ten minutes now, until I feel calmer.*

Using any of these alternative responses will help Jenny to feel less angry and to build confidence in her ability to manage anger as it comes up. In this next exercise, you will give some thought to your own anger and how you can plan to respond to angry feelings differently.

Exercise 9.5: Changing Angry Behavior

In this exercise, you will think about a time when you were angry and reacted to your anger in ways that were unhelpful. You will then come up with some alternative responses that you could have used. Thinking this through can prepare you to use healthier strategies the next time you feel angry.

When I felt angry…

The trigger was: _____

These thoughts went through my mind:

_____

_____

_____

_____

My unhealthy responses were: _____

_____

_____

_____

Some alternative, healthier responses might have been:

_____

_____

_____

_____

Coping with Negative Emotions

So far in this chapter, you've been practicing cognitive strategies for managing negative emotions—namely, identifying and challenging the thoughts that lead to them. This can be a very effective approach. But sometimes, for various reasons, a behavioral technique (in other words, *doing* something therapeutic rather than *thinking* your way through it) or a less time-intensive cognitive technique (like saying a quick reassuring phrase to yourself) may be a better choice for you. Here, we review a range of therapeutic strategies that you can try in the face of any negative feeling that might be triggering for you, whether it's anger, sadness, guilt, shame, anxiety, or another emotion.

- Try using the five-minute SOBER breathing exercise that you learned in chapter 7.

- Do something that relaxes you. A few ideas:

  - Focus on your breathing for a few minutes.

  - Go for a walk.

  - Take a bath.

  - Listen to some music.

- Try doing one of the pleasant activities you identified in exercise 8.3, in chapter 8. Remember that pleasant activities have a positive impact on your mood.

- Exercise. This can be a great outlet for negative emotions and the nervous energy that you might feel when you are worked up.

- Call someone you feel comfortable talking to. You don't even have to talk about what's bothering you if you don't want to. Sometimes just hearing the sound of a supportive voice can get you through a tough moment.

- Go to a self-help meeting.

- Say something reassuring to yourself. A lot of the time what gets and keeps us anxious or down is the feeling that we can't cope with things when they get to a certain point. But this isn't necessarily true. Try telling yourself:

  - *I can get through this.*

  - *I can handle this.*

  - *I can cope with whatever life sends my way.*

  - *I've made it this far; I just need to take things one day at a time, one moment at a time.*

  - *I don't have to say or do anything about how I am feeling right now. I can just get through this moment, and figure out what to do later.*

- Give yourself some credit. You are working your way through a difficult moment or day without drinking or using. You're using your intention to get through this in a healthy way to prevent yourself from spiraling into a relapse or reacting in some other self-destructive way that would make matters worse for yourself.

- Practice mindful acceptance. Sometimes, when circumstances that are upsetting to you are out of your control, entering a mode of acceptance can be the most therapeutic approach. Here are some things that you can tell yourself to find your way to acceptance:

- *This is just how it is right now.*

- *Even though I don't like this, I can tolerate it.*

- *I'm not going to judge the way I'm feeling. This is my experience. Maybe I can learn something from it.*

Revisit Your Motivation

No matter what it is that triggers an urge to drink or use, reminding yourself of the reasons that you are working so hard to stay sober can be a very effective tool to keep you on track with your recovery goals. This is no different when it comes to negative emotions. Go back to exercise 3.2 in chapter 3, Resolving Your Ambivalence, in which you explored the benefits and drawbacks of quitting versus continuing to drink or use. If you completed this exercise thoroughly, you should see something about relief from depression, anxiety, or any other triggering negative emotion for you as one of the benefits of continuing to drink or use. Now take a look at the drawbacks you listed of continuing to drink or use, along with the benefits of quitting. Any time you feel tempted by a negative emotion, you can revisit this exercise. After you've thought carefully about your reasons for quitting, then rate your motivation for sobriety on a scale from 0 to 10, with zero meaning that you are not motivated at all, and 10 meaning that you are as motivated as you can possibly be.

0	1	2	3	4	5	6	7	8	9	10
Not Motivated			Somewhat Motivated			Motivated			Highly Motivated	

Wherever you are on the scale, ask yourself what it would take to move one point higher. Keeping your motivation strong—partly by reminding yourself of the reasons you are going to all of this trouble to stay sober—will help you resist the temptation to drink or use when you are feeling down.

Wrap-up

Studies show that negative emotions are among the most common relapse triggers. The great news is, the most useful techniques for coping with negative emotions are the same as those that you've been using to cope with cravings to drink or use—such as challenging your thoughts, practicing mindfulness, learning acceptance, and engaging in pleasant activities. Now you just need to apply these strategies to your negative thoughts and feelings, as you've been practicing by using the exercises in this chapter.

By this point you've learned all of the essential skills that you need to manage the road to recovery. In the next and last chapter of this book, putting all of your hard work together, you will reflect on all that you've learned and—based on what you've observed to be the most helpful strategies—you will put together an integrated, personalized relapse prevention plan that you can use going forward in your recovery process.

CHAPTER 10

Your Personalized Recovery Plan

You've come a long way since you started this workbook. You have been practicing a lot of skills to help keep you sober and to pave the way to find happiness, pleasure, and emotional balance in your recovery. You understand the way your addicted brain works. You've strengthened your rational brain repeatedly with CBT skills, mindfulness training, motivational exercises, new sources of pleasure to replace drugs and alcohol, and a deeper understanding of how your unique relapse triggers lead you to drink or use. In this chapter, we're going to put all of the skills you've learned together into a personalized recovery plan that will help you stay happy, healthy, and sober in the long term.

There are a few ways that you will use the skills you've learned to prepare for long-term recovery. First, you will need to be aware of your personal warning signs for relapse, and be prepared with a plan for what to do if you or someone close to you begins to notice these signs becoming apparent. Second, although the hope is that you won't slip or relapse, given that most people who are in recovery do at one time or another, you will need to prepare for how to handle a slip, to prevent it from turning into a full-blown relapse. Finally, putting all of your hard work together, you will reflect on all that you've learned in this workbook and, based on what you've observed to be the most helpful strategies, you will put together an integrated, personalized relapse prevention plan that you can use going forward in your recovery process.

Staying One Step Ahead of a Relapse

The great news about where you are now, compared to when you started this workbook, is that you know exactly what triggers you and makes you vulnerable. Equipped with this knowledge, you're less likely to be blindsided by an urge to drink or use. You just have to pay attention to what's coming up ahead.

For at least the first six months of your recovery, one of the best ways to stay ahead of a potential relapse is to sit down at the start of each week and take the time to think about the days ahead. Do you know of any risky or potentially stressful situations coming up? (These could be family-related, work-related, or other situations that might result in the urge to drink or use.) If so, you can plan how you're going to handle them ahead of time. If you feel triggered, will you leave? Will you plan not to stay very long to begin with, so as to avoid getting triggered? Will you use a meditation technique? Maybe you'll bring someone with you who is sober. Or if it's possible, you'll consider avoiding that situation altogether.

These are just a few examples of plans that you can lay out if you take the time to think about what's coming up for you. It may be helpful to refer back to the Urge Planner in chapter 6. Plan on completing this exercise on a weekly basis for as long as you can (ideally, for the first six months of your recovery). You can discuss it with your counselor or therapist, if you have one, and get some input as to how to plan for potentially triggering situations.

Signs of Trouble

If you think back to the last time that you slipped or relapsed, there were probably warning signs before you entered the situation in which you actually drank or used. Recovery is not just about behaviors (such as avoiding risky situations, or going to therapy or self-help meetings)—as you well know now, it is also a mindset.

As the strength of your motivation for recovery naturally moves up and down, you may find yourself slipping out of the recovery mindset at times. Although this does not necessarily mean that you are headed straight for a relapse, it is best to be aware when it is happening so that you can take steps to renew your motivation and get yourself back on track. In exercise 11.1, you'll find a list of some common warning signs. These signs can relate to either your mindset or your behaviors. As you look through this list, think about times when you've relapsed; in the days and even the weeks before, you probably experienced some changes in the way you were thinking about your recovery, or the way you were acting or feeling emotionally. Maybe you didn't realize at the time that these warning signs were there, but now as you look back on it, things may become a little bit clearer.

Exercise 11.1: My Warning Signs of Relapse

Look at the list of warning signs below and place a check mark beside the ones that you can identify with, or that you've observed in yourself prior to a relapse.

_____   Stopping or cutting back your attendance in therapy or counseling

_____   Thinking about ways that you might be able to drink or use without anyone knowing about it

_____   Fantasizing often about how good it would feel to drink or use, while blocking out or thinking very little about the potential negative consequences

_____   Stopping or cutting back your attendance in self-help groups, such as AA or SMART Recovery

_____   Isolating yourself

_____   Placing yourself in risky situations

_____   Avoiding talking about mixed feelings or doubts you have about staying sober

_____   Starting to use a drug other than your "substance of choice"

_____   Feeling intense negative emotions, such as depression, anxiety, anger, or irritability

_____   Feeling that you don't fit in with others who are in recovery

_____   Blaming other people for your problems

_____   Having very few activities that are fun or enjoyable in your routine

_____   Not sleeping well or not sleeping enough

_____   Neglecting responsibilities, such as paying bills, doing household tasks, taking care of loved ones, or getting to work or school

_____   Avoiding talking about feelings of unhappiness

_____ Feeling hopeless about your ability to rebuild your life

_____ Keeping alcohol, drugs, or paraphernalia at home

_____ Hanging on to phone numbers of dealers or people you used to use with

_____ Lying

_____ Rejecting help from others

_____ Feeling bored or having lots of unstructured or unplanned time

_____ Spending time with people who drink or use

_____ Acting defensive when others around you express concern about your well-being or recovery

Other relapse warning signs:

_____

_____

_____

Now, looking back at the list, identify which you think are the top three signs that you are at risk of relapse. You will need a plan for what you will do if you or someone close to you points out any of these signs. Here are some examples of potential plans:

- Discuss it with your therapist or counselor, if you have one.

- Seek to start or resume therapy or counseling, if you're not currently attending.

- Consult with a psychiatrist to evaluate whether medications are needed to manage any psychological symptoms (such as depression or anxiety).

- Increase your attendance at self-help meetings.

- Call your 12-step sponsor if you have one, or seek out a sponsor.

- Review relevant exercises in this workbook related to strengthening your motivation, challenging your thoughts, and increasing pleasant activities.

- Initiate an exercise plan, or step up your existing one.

You might come up with other ideas. But this list can help you begin to think about how you can respond to your warning signs.

My Top Three Warning Signs of Relapse:

Warning sign #1: _____

Plan if I notice this sign: _____

_____

Warning sign #2: _____

Plan if I notice this sign: _____

_____

Warning sign #3: _____

Plan if I notice this sign: _____

_____

Put a Stop to the Slip

You might remember our discussion about the difference between a "slip" and a relapse. To review here briefly, the first time you drink or use after a period of being sober or abstinent, it is called a "slip." Although you may be committed to abstinence, and it might be hard to imagine that you'd slip, studies of addiction have shown that the tendency to return to substance use after a period of sobriety is part of the illness (NIDA 2010). So it is best to be prepared for the possibility that this could happen.

The important thing to remember is that your response to a slip makes all the difference in terms of the impact it has on your recovery. A slip doesn't have to set you back tremendously, if you're willing to address it immediately by: (1) talking about it with a counselor, therapist, or sponsor; (2) figuring out what went wrong; and (3) putting safeguards into place to prevent it from progressing into a relapse. A relapse happens when you allow a slip to lead to an extended period of days, weeks, or longer during which you actively drink or use drugs. Here are some things that you can tell yourself to prevent a slip from heading in the relapse direction:

- *I can leave the slip behind me as long as I don't repeat it.*

- *I can use the slip as a learning opportunity. If I understand why it happened, I can prevent it from happening again.*

- *I may feel bad about it, but that will pass. As long as I get right back on the road to recovery, without wasting any more time drinking or using, I will feel good about myself again very soon.*

Another important thing to remember is to catch yourself if you find that you are getting into the *spiraling lapse* mindset. In chapter 5, we discussed how sometimes when you experience a slip or a lapse, it can trigger dysfunctional thoughts like, *I've blown it. I'm a total failure. I'll never stay sober. I have nothing to lose by continuing to drink (or use).* Beware of the spiraling lapse frame of mind; it is a sure pathway from a slip to a full-blown relapse. You can avoid it by recognizing it for what it is, and intentionally bringing your thoughts into a more CBT-oriented mindset, in which you view the slip as a learning opportunity that you can quickly move past.

Once you've preserved your recovery mindset, brought yourself out of the spiraling lapse mode, accepted that the slip happened, and decided that you are ready to put it behind you, there are a few more steps you can take to prevent any further drug or alcohol use:

- Go back to chapter 3 and revisit your motivation to stay sober. Pay particular attention to exercises 3.2, on the benefits and drawbacks of quitting versus continuing to drink or use, and 3.3, on ways to strengthen your motivation. Understanding the importance of renewing your motivation often is a key part of successful recovery and keeping your rational mind in control.

- Learn from the situation. Find someone—preferably a therapist or counselor—to review the sequence of events leading to the relapse and help you figure out what went wrong. This will involve considering the following questions:

  - Were there any warning signs over the past few days, weeks, or months?

  - Did you address the warning signs? If so, what more could you have done? If not, why not?

  - How did you end up in the situation in which you relapsed?

  - What was the trigger?

  - How did the relapse affect you?

  - How can you cope more effectively the next time you are confronted with a similar situation or trigger?

- Step up the support. A slip is a sign that one or more parts of your recovery plan were not firmly in place. Sometimes stepping up the social or professional support for your recovery can help solidify your relapse prevention program. This could take the form of:

  - More involvement in self-help groups

  - Getting into therapy or increasing the frequency of therapy

  - More social contact with people in recovery (like having coffee with sober friends, or making more efforts to connect with others who are in recovery)

  - Considering medication treatment for your addiction or mental health if you aren't receiving any, or discussing a change to your current medication treatment with your provider.

Your Personalized Relapse Prevention Plan

Now that you've worked your way through all of the chapters and the exercises in each one, you are well positioned to manage your recovery both now and in the long term. In each of the chapters, you've been trying new skills and, hopefully, making mental notes about which of them have been most helpful to you.

In this section you're going to revisit these skills and mark off the ones that you think you'd like to use, going forward in your recovery. Some of the skills are general recovery lifestyle behaviors; they keep you feeling happy and balanced, reducing your risk of a relapse. (Examples include doing pleasant activities, exercising, and communicating effectively with others.) Other coping skills that you've learned are more specific to risky situations (like surfing the urge, the mindfulness-based SOBER breathing exercise, and challenging red flag thoughts). Reflecting on the skills you've learned in this program, place a check mark beside those that you found helpful:

Motivation Enhancing Skills

_____ Thinking about what stage of change you're in, rating your current motivation to quit (from 0 to 10), and thinking about what it would take to move your motivation rating up by at least one point

_____ Reviewing the benefits and drawbacks of continuing to drink or use, as well as the benefits and drawbacks of quitting

_____ Reviewing the problems that alcohol or drug use have caused in your life

_____ Thinking about what concerns you about your alcohol or drug use, and what you can imagine happening if you were to continue drinking or using

_____ Thinking about how quitting has affected and will continue to affect your life

_____ Reviewing the reasons why you believe you have the ability to get and stay sober

General Wellness Skills

_____ Being aware of seemingly irrelevant decisions

_____ Selecting and committing to an exercise activity

_____ Keeping an exercise log

_____ Rewarding yourself for following through on your exercise plans

_____ Identifying the Safety Nets in your social and family life, as well as risky relationships

_____ Using assertive communication to make recovery-related requests from others and to refuse offers of alcohol or drugs

_____ Expanding your social network in one or more ways

_____ Keeping a schedule

_____ Identifying and scheduling pleasant activities that are incompatible with drinking and using

_____ Rewarding yourself for following through with pleasant activities

Alcohol- and Drug-Specific Coping Skills

_____ Identifying your triggers

_____ Being aware of your red flag thoughts

_____ Recognizing and challenging mistakes in thinking

_____ Monitoring your triggers and cravings

_____ Getting rid of all alcohol, drugs, and paraphernalia

_____ Surfing the urge to cope with a craving

_____ Distracting yourself to cope with a craving

_____ Delaying the decision to drink or use by fifteen minutes to cope with a craving

_____ Using the Urge Planner to anticipate and plan for risky situations

_____ Using mindfulness exercises to develop a meditation practice

_____ Using the SOBER mindfulness exercise to cope with a craving

_____ Practicing mindful acceptance

_____ Getting involved (or more involved) in mutual self-help groups, like AA or SMART Recovery

Mood and Anger Management

_____ Monitoring your mood and cravings

_____ Monitoring your anxiety and cravings

_____ Identifying and challenging negative thoughts that lead to anxiety and depression

_____ Identifying anger triggers

_____ Practicing "giving it a beat" when you're angry

_____ Challenging angry thoughts

Now, you will list the skills in each category that you plan to use as your "go-to" strategies in your personalized relapse prevention plan. Think about which exercises have spoken the most to you and your personal experience. Also think about which of the techniques you have found yourself using when you were not reading this workbook, but just out living your life and navigating challenges in your recovery.

When I need to enhance my motivation for recovery, I will use the following techniques:

1. _____

2. _____

3. _____

The general wellness skills that I plan to continue using in my recovery include:

1. _____

2. _____

3. _____

4. _____

5. _____

6. _____

The alcohol- and drug-specific coping skills that I plan to use when I am tempted to drink or use are:

1. _____

2. _____

3. _____

4. _____

5. _____

6. _____

People I can call if I am tempted to drink or use include:

1. _____

2. _____

3. _____

The mood and anger management techniques that I will continue to use include:

1. _____

2. _____

3. _____

Other skills I plan to use going forward in my recovery:

1. _____

2. _____

3. _____

Wrap-up

Congratulations on your hard work and persistence throughout this workbook. You've taken in a lot of new information about the science of addiction, and you've tried out many different types of coping skills. In doing so, you've laid the essential groundwork for your ongoing recovery.

You now have a range of evidence-based therapy techniques that are used in addiction treatment at your fingertips, and you have the flexibility to choose which ones you'd like to use, based on the relapse prevention plan that you've laid out in this final chapter. You've made great strides in developing the tools that you need to live a well-balanced and happy life in your recovery. Keep up your hard work; you are well on your way toward rebuilding a satisfying and rewarding life, free from alcohol and drugs.

Acknowledgments

This book would not have been possible without the support and guidance of many to whom I am deeply grateful. Several of my most influential teachers throughout my training as a clinician and scientist enabled me to become the expert that I am in the various therapy approaches to the treatment of addiction that are integrated in this book, and I am deeply grateful to them: Bruce Overmier, Sandra Brown, John McQuaid, and Tamara Wall. I am profoundly appreciative for the mentorship of Thomas Mintz, who inspired me with his wisdom and knowledge about how to synthesize my scientific expertise and clinical experience to form a book that could reach addicted clients directly.

The idea that formed the basis of this book—that integrating the various evidence-based therapeutic approaches to addiction treatment and providing them in a single source could enable those with addictions to individualize their approach to recovery—was born out of a series of conversations with Richard Rawson, to whom I owe an enormous debt of gratitude for helping me form and crystallize my ideas, and for fueling my passion for addiction science and treatment throughout my career.

I have valued greatly the professionalism and skills of Tesilya Hanauer and her colleagues at New Harbinger, who contributed to the development and production of this book, including Jess Beebe, Marisa Solís, and Angela Autry Gorden, as well as freelance editor Susan LaCroix. To Hélène Chokron Garneau at UCLA, I extend a special thank-you for her dedication to my clinical research and tireless efforts in the process of assembling this workbook. I'd also like to gratefully acknowledge the help and support of the agencies that have funded my research on developing and evaluating behavioral treatments for addictions and related conditions: the National Institute on Drug Abuse and the National Institute on Alcoholism and Alcohol Abuse.

It is a pleasure to thank the many clients I have worked with over the years who have helped me understand the psychology of addiction and the struggles that are at the core of recovery.

Finally, I am forever grateful to my family for their love and support throughout the process of bringing this project to fruition; I know how lucky I am.

Resources

Drug Facts

http://easyread.drugabuse.gov/

Cognitive Behavioral Therapy

Information about finding a certified specialist: http://www.beckinstituteblog
  .org/2007/03/cognitive-behavior-therapist-how-to-find-one/

Frequently asked questions about CBT:
  www.beckinstitute.org/cognitive-behavioral-therapy/

CBT tools and resources: www.beckinstitute.org/cbtstore/

List of books that discuss CBT and substance abuse:
  www.beckinstitute.org/cbtstore/cbt-books/#substance

Therapist Finders:

http://locator.apa.org/

http://www.abctcentral.org/xFAT/

http://www.nacbt.org/searchfortherapists.ASP

http://members.academyofct.org (click on "Find a Therapist")

Addiction Medicine

Find an addiction medicine professional:
http://community.asam.org/search/default.asp?m=basic

American Society of Addiction Medicine's page for the public:
http://www.asam.org/for-the-public

Mindfulness

UCLA Mindful Awareness Research Center: http://marc.ucla.edu/

Find a mindfulness-based addiction therapist:
http://www.mindfulrp.com/For-Clients.html

Listen to audio recordings of practices used in Mindfulness-Based Relapse
Prevention: http://www.mindfulrp.com/For-Clients.html

UCSD Center for Mindfulness: https://ucsdcfm.wordpress.com/

Mindful: http://www.mindful.org/

Book about mindfulness for addiction: Bowen, Chawla, and Marlatt (2010).
Mindfulness-Based Relapse Prevention for Addictive Behaviors: A Clinician's Guide. New
York: Guilford Press.

Harm Reduction

Harm Reduction Coalition: http://www.harmreduction.org

Alan Marlatt on Harm Reduction Therapy: http://www.psychotherapy.net
/interview/marlatt-harm-reduction

Book about harm reduction: Marlatt, Larimer, and Witkiewitz (2011). *Harm
Reduction, Second Edition: Pragmatic Strategies for Managing High-Risk Behaviors.* New
York: Guilford Press.

References

American Psychiatric Association. 2013. *Diagnostic and Statistical Manual of Mental Disorders.* 5th ed. Arlington, VA: American Psychiatric Publishing.

Annis, H. M., and C. S. Davis. 1989. "Relapse Prevention Training: A Cognitive-Behavioral Approach Based on Self-Efficacy Theory." *Journal of Chemical Dependency Treatment* 2(2): 81–103.

Astin, J. A. 1997. "Stress Reduction Through Mindfulness Meditation: Effects on Psychological Symptomatology, Sense of Control, and Spiritual Experiences." *Psychotherapy and Psychosomatics* 66(2): 97–106.

Bowen, S., N. Chawla, and G. A. Marlatt. 2010. *Mindfulness-Based Relapse Prevention for Addictive Behaviors: A Clinician's Guide.* New York: Guilford Press.

Bowen, S., K. Witkiewitz, S. L. Clifasefi, J. Grow, N. Chawla, S. H. Hsu, H. A. Carroll, E. Harrop, S. E. Collins, K. Lustyk, and M. E. Larimer. 2014. "Relative Efficacy of Mindfulness-Based Relapse Prevention, Standard Relapse Prevention, and Treatment as Usual for Substance Use Disorders." *JAMA Psychiatry* 71(5): 547–56.

Breslin, F. C., M. Zack, and S. McMain. 2002. "An Information-Processing Analysis of Mindfulness: Implications for Relapse Prevention in the Treatment of Substance Abuse." *Clinical Psychology: Science and Practice* 9(3), 275–99.

Brown, S. A., S. V. Glasner-Edwards, S. R. Tate, J. R. McQuaid, J. Chalekian, and E. Granholm. 2006. "Integrated Cognitive Behavioral Therapy Versus Twelve-Step Facilitation for Substance Dependent Adults with Depressive Disorders." *Journal of Psychoactive Drugs* 38(4): 449–60.

Budney, A. J., B. A. Moore, H. L. Rocha, and S. T. Higgins. 2006. "Clinical Trial of Abstinence-Based Vouchers and Cognitive-Behavioral Therapy for Cannabis Dependence." *Journal of Consulting and Clinical Psychology* 74(2): 307–16.

Carlson, L. E., M. Speca, K. D. Patel, and E. Goodey. 2004. "Mindfulness-Based Stress Reduction in Relation to Quality of Life, Mood, Symptoms of Stress and Levels of Cortisol, Dehydroepiandrosterone Sulfate (DHEAS) and Melatonin in Breast and Prostate Cancer Outpatients." *Psychoneuroendocrinology* 29(4): 448–74.

Centers for Disease Control. 2015. "How Much Physical Activity Do Adults Need?" Retrieved from http://www.cdc.gov/physicalactivity/everyone/guidelines/adults.html.

Childress A. R., R. N. Ehrman, Z. Wang, Y. Li, N. Sciortino, J. Hakun, W. Jens, J. Suh, J. Listerud, K. Marquez, T. Franklin, D. Langleben, J. Detre, and C. P. O'Brien. 2008. "Prelude to Passion: Limbic Activation by Unseen Drug and Sexual Cues." *PLoS ONE* 3(1): e1506.

Church S. H., J. L. Rothenberg, M. A. Sullivan, G. Bornstein, and E. V. Nunes. 2001. "Concurrent Substance Use and Outcome in Combined Behavioral and Naltrexone Therapy for Opiate Dependence." *American Journal of Drug and Alcohol Abuse* 27: 441–452.

Cuijpers, P., F. Smit, and A. van Straten. 2007. "Psychological Treatments of Subthreshold Depression: A Metaanalytic Review." *Acta Psychiatrica Scandinavica* 115(6), 434–41.

Daughters, S.B., A. R. Braun, M. N. Sargeant, E. K. Reynolds, D. E. Hopko, C. Blanco, and C. W. Lejuez. 2008. "Effectiveness of a Brief Behavioral Treatment for Inner-City Illicit Drug Users with Elevated Depressive Symptoms: The Life Enhancement Treatment for Substance Use (LETS ACT!)." *Journal of Clinical Psychiatry* 69, 122–29.

DeVito, E. E., P. D. Worhunsky, K. M. Carroll, B. J. Rounsaville, H. Kober, and M. N. Potenza. 2012. "A Preliminary Study of the Neural Effects of Behavioral Therapy for Substance Use Disorders." *Drug and Alcohol Dependence* 122(3): 228–235.

Di Chiara, G., and A. Imperato. 1988. "Drugs Abused by Humans Preferentially Increase Synaptic Dopamine Concentrations in the Mesolimbic System of Freely Moving Rats." *Proceedings of the National Academy of Sciences* 85(14): 5274–8.

Dobson, K. S. 2013. "The Science of CBT: Toward a Metacognitive Model of Change?" *Behavior Therapy* 44(2): 224–27.

Dolezal, B. A., J. Chudzynski, T. W. Storer, M. Abrazado, J. Penate, L. Mooney, D. Dickerson, R. A. Rawson, and C. B. Cooper. 2013. "Eight Weeks of Exercise Training Improves Fitness Measures in Methamphetamine-Dependent Individuals in Residential Treatment." *Journal of Addiction Medicine* 7(2): 122–28.

Enoch, M. 2012. "The Influence of Gene-Environment Interactions on the Development of Alcoholism and Drug Dependence." *Current Psychiatry Reports* 14(2): 150–58.

Epstein, E. E. and B. S. McCrady. 2009. *Overcoming Alcohol Use Problems: A Cognitive-Behavioral Treatment Program.* New York: Oxford University Press.

Evans, S., S. Ferrando, M. Findler, C. Stowell, C. Smart, and D. Haglin. 2008. "Mindfulness-Based Cognitive Therapy for Generalized Anxiety Disorder." *Journal of Anxiety Disorders* 22(4): 716–21.

Farabee, D., R. Rawson, and M. McCann. 2002. "Adoption of Drug Avoidance Activities Among Patients in Contingency Management and Cognitive-Behavioral Treatments." *Journal of Substance Abuse Treatment* 23: 343–50.

Glasner-Edwards, S., P. Marinelli-Casey, R. Gonzales, M. Hillhouse, A. Ang, L. J. Mooney, and R. Rawson. 2009. "Depression Among Methamphetamine Users: Association with Outcomes from the Methamphetamine Treatment Project at Three-Year Follow-Up." *Journal of Nervous and Mental Disease* 197: 225–31.

Glasner-Edwards, S. L. J. Mooney, A. Ang, H. C. Garneau, E. Hartwell, M. Brecht, and R. A. Rawson. Forthcoming. "Mindfulness-Based Relapse Prevention for Stimulant Dependent Adults: A Pilot Randomized Clinical Trial." *Addiction.*

Glasner-Edwards, S., L. J. Mooney, A. Ang, M. Hillhouse, and R. Rawson. 2013. "Does Post-Traumatic Stress Disorder Affect Post-Treatment Methamphetamine Use?" *Journal of Dual Diagnosis* 9(2): 123–28.

Green, L., and J. H. Kagel, (Eds.) 1996. *Advances in Behavioral Economics, Vol. 3: Substance Use and Abuse.* Norwood, NJ: Ablex.

Hanson, G. R. 2002. "New Insights into Relapse." *NIDA Notes* 17:3. National Institute on Drug Abuse. National Institute of Health. U.S. Department of Health and Human Services.

Hettema, J., J. Steele, and W. R. Miller. 2005. "Motivational Interviewing." *Annual Review of Clinical Psychology* 1: 91–111.

Higgins, S. T., S. M. Alessi, and R. L. Dantona. 2002. "Voucher-Based Incentives. A Substance Abuse Treatment Innovation." *Addictive Behaviors* 27(6): 887–910.

Kabat-Zinn J., A. O. Massion, J. Kristeller, L. G. Peterson, K. E. Fletcher, L. Pbert, W. R. Lenderking, and S. F. Santorelli. 1992. "Effectiveness of a Meditation-Based Stress Reduction Program in the Treatment of Anxiety Disorders." *American Journal of Psychiatry* 149(7): 936–43.

Kabat-Zinn J. 1982. "An Outpatient Program in Behavioral Medicine for Chronic Pain Patients Based on the Practice of Mindfulness Meditation: Theoretical Considerations and Preliminary Results." *General Hospital Psychiatry* 4(1): 33–47.

Kabat-Zinn, J. 1990. *Full Catastrophe Living: Using the Wisdom of Your Body and Mind to Face Stress, Pain, and Illness.* New York: Delacorte.

Kabat-Zinn, J. 2003. "Mindfulness-Based Interventions in Context: Past, Present, and Future." *Clinical Psychology: Science and Practice* 10(2): 144–56.

Kelly, J. F., and M.C. Greene. 2014. "Where There's a Will There's a Way: A Longitudinal Investigation of the Interplay Between Recovery Motivation and Self-Efficacy in Predicting Treatment Outcome." *Psychology of Addictive Behaviors* 28(3): 928–34.

Kelly, J. F., B. Hoeppner, R. L. Stout, and M. Pagano. 2012. "Determining the Relative Importance of the Mechanisms of Behavior Change Within Alcoholics Anonymous: A Multiple Mediator Analysis." *Addiction* 107: 289–99.

Kendler, K. S., L. M Karkowski, M. C. Neale, and C. A. Prescott. 2000. "Illicit Psychoactive Substance Use, Heavy Use, Abuse, and Dependence in a US Population-Based Sample of Male Twins." *Archives of General Psychiatry* 57: 261–69.

Larimer, M. E., R. S. Palmer, and G. A. Marlatt. 1999. "Relapse Prevention. An Overview of Marlatt's Cognitive-Behavioral Model." *Alcohol Research and Health* 23(2): 151–60.

Magidson, J. F., S. M. Gorka, L. MacPherson, D. R. Hopko, C. Blanco, C. W. Lejuez, and S. B. Daughters. 2011. "Examining the Effect of the Life Enhancement Treatment for Substance Use (LETS ACT) on Residential Substance Abuse Treatment Retention." *Addictive Behaviors* 36(6), 615–23.

Marlatt, G. A., and J. R. Gordon (Eds). 1985. *Relapse Prevention: Maintenance Strategies in the Treatment of Addictive Behaviors.* New York: Guilford Press.

Marlatt, G. A. 1996. "Taxonomy of High-Risk Situations for Alcohol Relapse: Evolution and Development of a Cognitive-Behavioral Model." *Addiction* 91(suppl): 37–49.

Marlatt, G. A. and B. D. Ostafin. 2005. "Being Mindful of Automaticity in Addiction: A Clinical Perspective." In *Handbook of Implicit Cognition and Addiction*, edited by R. W. Wiers and A. W. Stacy. Thousand Oaks, CA: Sage.

Mazzucchelli, T., R. Kane, and C. Rees. 2009. "Behavioral Activation Treatments for Depression in Adults: A Meta-Analysis and Review." *Clinical Psychology: Science and Practice* 16(4), 383–411.

McAuliffe W. E. 1990. "A Randomized Control Trial of Recovery Training for Opioid Addicts in New England and Hong Kong." *Journal of Psychoactive Drugs* 22: 197–209.

McLellan, A. T., D. C. Lewis, C. P. O'Brien, and H. D. Kleber. 2000. "Drug Dependence, a Chronic Medical Illness: Implications for Treatment, Insurance, and Outcomes Evaluation." *JAMA.* 284(13): 1689–95.

Miller, W. R. 1983. "Motivational Interviewing with Problem Drinkers." *Behavioral Psychotherapy 11*: 147–72.

Miller, W. R. 1996. "Motivational Interviewing: Research, Practice, and Puzzles." *Addictive Behaviors* 21(6), 835–42.

Mooney, L.J., Cooper, C., London, E.D., Chudzynski, J., Dolezal, B., Dickerson, D., Brecht, M.L., Penate, J., and Rawson, R.A. (2014). Exercise for methamphetamine dependence: rationale, design, and methodology. *Contemporary Clinical Trials,* 37(1): 139–47.

Morgenstern, J., E. Labouvie, B. S. McCrady, C. W. Kahler, and R. M. Frey. 1997. "Affiliation with Alcoholics Anonymous After Treatment: A Study of Its Therapeutic Effects and Mechanisms of Action." *Journal of Consulting and Clinical Psychology* 65: 768–77.

NIDA (National Institute on Drug Abuse). 2010. *Drugs, Brains, and Behavior: The Science of Addiction.* NIH Pub No. 10–5605.

Pollack, M. H., S. A. Penava, E. Bolton, J. J. Worthington III, G. L. Allen, F. J. Farach, and M. W. Otto. 2002. "A Novel Cognitive-Behavioral Approach for Treatment-Resistant Drug Dependence." *Journal of Substance Abuse Treatment* 23: 335–42.

Prochaska, J. O., C. C. DiClemente, and J. C. Norcross. 1992. "In Search of How People Change: Applications to Addictive Behaviors." *American Psychologist* 47(9): 1102–14.

Ramel, W., P. R. Goldin, P. E. Carmona, and J. R. McQuaid. 2004. "The Effects of Mindfulness Meditation on Cognitive Processes and Affect in Patients with Past Depression." *Cognitive Therapy and Research* 28(4): 433–55.

Rawson R. A., J. Chudzynski, L. Mooney, R. Gonzales, A. Ang, D. Dickerson, J. Penate, B. A. Salem, B. Dolezal, and C. B. Cooper. 2015. "Impact of an Exercise Intervention on Methamphetamine Use Outcomes Post-Residential Treatment Care." *Drug and Alcohol Dependence*. Under review.

Rawson, R. A., P. Marinelli-Casey, M. D. Anglin, A. Dickow, Y. Frazier, C. Gallagher, G. P. Galloway, J. Herrell, A. Huber, M. J. McCann, J. Obert, S. Pennell, C. Reiber, D. Vandersloot, and J. Zweben. 2004. "A Multi-Site Comparison of Psychosocial Approaches for the Treatment of Methamphetamine Dependence." *Addiction* 99(6): 708–17.

Roemer, L., and S. M. Orsillo. 2003. "Mindfulness: A Promising Intervention Strategy in Need of Further Study." *Clinical Psychology: Science and Practice* 10(2): 172–78.

Rohsenow, D. J., P. M. Monti, R. A. Martin, S. M. Colby, M. G. Myers, S. B. Gulliver, R. A. Brown, T. I. Mueller, A. Gordon, and D. B. Abrams. 2004. "Motivational Enhancement and Coping Skills Training for Cocaine Abusers: Effects on Substance Use Outcomes." *Addiction* 99(7): 862–74.

Shapiro, S. L., G. E. Schwartz, and G. Bonner. 1998. "Effects of Mindfulness-Based Stress Reduction on Medical and Premedical Students." *Journal of Behavioral Medicine* 21(6): 581–99.

Sheff, D. 2014. "How Philip Seymour Hoffman Could Have Been Saved." *Time*, Feb 2. Retrieved from http://time.com/3390/how-philip-seymour-hoffman-could-have-been-saved/

Sinha R. 2007. "The Role of Stress in Addiction Relapse." *Current Psychiatry Reports* 9: 388–95.

Sinha, R. 2008. "Chronic Stress, Drug Use, and Vulnerability to Addiction." *Annals of the New York Academy of Sciences* 1141, 105–30.

Stein M. D., D. S. Herman, D. A. Solomon, J. L. Anthony, B. J. Anderson, S. E. Ramsey, and I. W. Miller. 2004. "Adherence to Treatment of Depression in Active Injection Drug Users: The Minerva Study." *Journal of Substance Abuse Treatment* 26, 87–93.

Sturmey, P. 2009. "Behavioral Activation Is an Evidence-Based Treatment for Depression." *Behavior Modification* 33(6), 818–29.

Tate, S. R., J. Wu, J. R. McQuaid, K. Cummins, C. Shriver, M. Krenek, and S. A. Brown. 2008. "Comorbidity of Substance Dependence and Depression: Role of Life Stress and Self-Efficacy in Sustaining Abstinence." *Psychology of Addictive Behaviors* 22(1): 47–57.

Timko, C., R. Billow, and A. DeBenedetti. 2006. "Determinants of 12-step Group Affiliation and Moderators of the Affiliation-Abstinence Relationship." *Drug and Alcohol Dependence* 83(2): 111–21.

Tsuang, M. T., M. J. Lyons, J. M. Meyer, T. Doyle, S. A. Eisen, J. Goldberg, W. True, N. Lin, R. Toomey, and L. Eaves. 1998. "Co-Occurrence of Abuse of Different Drugs in Men: The Role of Drug-Specific and Shared Vulnerabilities." *Archives of General Psychiatry* 55(11): 967–72.

Tsuang M. T., W. M. Stone, and S. V. Faraone. 2001. "Genes, Environment, and Schizophrenia." *British Journal of Psychiatry* 178(40): s18–s24.

Volkow, N.D., L. Chang, G. Wang, J. S. Fowler, D. Franceschi, M. Sedler, S. J. Gatley, E. Miller, R. Hitzemann, Y. Ding, and J. Logan. 2001. "Loss of Dopamine Transporters in Methamphetamine Abusers Recovers with Protracted Abstinence." *Journal of Neruoscience* 21(23): 9414–18.

Williams, K. A., M. M. Kolar, B. E. Reger, and J. C. Pearson. 2001. "Evaluation of a Wellness-Based Mindfulness Stress Reduction Intervention: A Controlled Trial." *American Journal of Health Promotion* 15(6): 422–32.

Witkiewitz K., M. K. Lustyk, and S. Bowen. 2013. "Retraining the Addicted Brain: A Review of Hypothesized Neurobiological Mechanisms of Mindfulness-Based Relapse Prevention." *Psychology of Addictive Behaviors* 27(2): 351–65.

Suzette Glasner Edwards, PhD, is associate professor of psychiatry at the University of California, Los Angeles (UCLA). As a principal investigator at the UCLA Integrated Substance Abuse Programs, her NIH-funded research in the area of behavioral treatments for addictions is widely published. She also maintains a private practice where she specializes in the use of cognitive behavioral, motivational, and mindfulness-based techniques to treat addictions and mental health problems.

Foreword writer **Richard A. Rawson, PhD**, is professor in residence in the department of psychiatry at the University of California, Los Angeles (UCLA), and codirector of the UCLA Integrated Substance Abuse Programs. He has worked in the substance abuse field since 1974. Rawson started the Matrix Institute on Addictions and conducts training on topics including basic principles of addiction and addiction treatment for counselors, MFCCs, psychologists, and physicians, and much more.

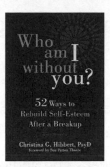
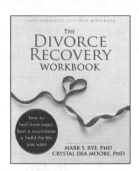
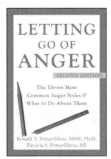
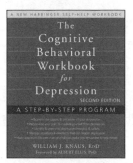
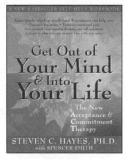

Register your **new harbinger** titles for additional benefits!

When you register your **new harbinger** title—purchased in any format, from any source—you get access to benefits like the following:

- Downloadable accessories like printable worksheets and extra content

- Instructional videos and audio files

- Information about updates, corrections, and new editions

Not every title has accessories, but we're adding new material all the time.

Access free accessories in 3 easy steps:

1. Sign in at NewHarbinger.com (or **register** to create an account).

2. Click on **register a book**. Search for your title and click the **register** button when it appears.

3. Click on the **book cover or title** to go to its details page. Click on **accessories** to view and access files.

That's all there is to it!

If you need help, visit:

NewHarbinger.com/accessories

new harbinger
CELEBRATING
40 YEARS